Digital Degrowth

Digital Degrowth
Radically Rethinking our Digital Futures

Neil Selwyn

polity

Copyright © Neil Selwyn 2025

The right of Neil Selwyn to be identified as Author of this Work has been asserted in accordance with the UK Copyright, Designs and Patents Act 1988.

First published in 2025 by Polity Press

Polity Press
65 Bridge Street
Cambridge CB2 1UR, UK

Polity Press
111 River Street
Hoboken, NJ 07030, USA

All rights reserved. Except for the quotation of short passages for the purpose of criticism and review, no part of this publication may be reproduced, stored in a retrieval system or transmitted, in any form or by any means, electronic, mechanical, photocopying, recording or otherwise, without the prior permission of the publisher.

ISBN-13: 978-1-5095-6327-2
ISBN-13: 978-1-5095-6328-9(pb)

A catalogue record for this book is available from the British Library.

Library of Congress Control Number: 2024948773

Typeset in 10.5/12pt Sabon LT Pro
by Cheshire Typesetting Ltd, Cuddington, Cheshire
Printed and bound in Great Britain by CPI Group (UK) Ltd, Croydon

The publisher has used its best endeavours to ensure that the URLs for external websites referred to in this book are correct and active at the time of going to press. However, the publisher has no responsibility for the websites and can make no guarantee that a site will remain live or that the content is or will remain appropriate.

Every effort has been made to trace all copyright holders, but if any have been overlooked the publisher will be pleased to include any necessary credits in any subsequent reprint or edition.

For further information on Polity, visit our website:
politybooks.com

Contents

1 The Need for Digital Change	1
2 Does Tech Have Any Solutions?	24
3 Beginning to Think Differently About Digital Technology	40
4 The Case for Digital Degrowth	57
5 Finding Alternatives in the Here and Now	76
6 Future Innovations	94
7 Where Now? Everywhere But Here!	108
References	124
Index	135

1
The Need for Digital Change

Introduction

It is time to start talking in earnest about the societal and environmental impacts of digital technology. More specifically, it is time to start calling out the harmful ways in which large parts of the planet are now bound up in an excess of digital devices, digital infrastructures and digitizations of everyday life. We live in a world where there are considerably more smartphones than people. We have reached a point where many important parts of our societies, cultures and economies have been rearranged along digital lines. Crucially, this defining presence of digital technology is impacting in material as well as virtual ways. The billions of digital devices scattered across our planet are constructed from rare minerals and metals that are fast depleting. Some of the most remote places on earth are struggling to accommodate resource-hungry data warehouses that are stuffed full of thousands of computer servers, while our oceans are littered with hundreds of undersea internet cables. All told, it feels that the world is being steadily suffocated by this planetary scale of computing.

These burdens and harms have tended to be rarely noticed – let alone mentioned – in mainstream discussions of the 'digital age'. As far as most people are concerned, digitization is something that is now so ubiquitous it no longer merits special attention. Yet, outside of mainstream media, policy and industry circles, calls are beginning to be made to break the hold that digital technology has over our lives and environments. While smartphones, AI and streaming might seem essential elements of modern life, we need to start thinking *beyond* the digital age. In a world of finite planetary resources and failing climate systems, it seems clear that digital technology cannot continue to expand indefinitely. The age of digital excess is fast losing momentum and appeal . . . let us look forward to an age of digital degrowth.

How digital technology became too big

Before we can start thinking expansively about digital futures it is useful to give a little thought to the digital present and past. This opening chapter takes time to map out the full extent of the intensive, excessive and profoundly harmful forms of digital technology that have come to pervade everyday life. Of course, some people contend that the distinction between 'digital' and 'non-digital' is no longer necessary given the near ubiquity of digital technologies throughout contemporary life. Yet this ignores many significant – and troubling – ways in which our dependency on digital technology has soured over the past few decades. This book starts from the premise that, now more than ever, it is important to talk explicitly and honestly about the digital.

The 'digital age' that we are currently experiencing is profoundly different from even ten years ago. The digital technologies of the 2020s are predicated upon overwhelming presence, conspicuous consumption and 'always-on' modes of operation. This is evident, for example, in how digital devices and platforms are now woven tightly into the fabric of daily life – an underpinning feature of everything from parenting children to managing household finances. It is commonplace for people's most intimate and private moments to be mediated through screens and algorithms. At the same time, most of the major institutions that define contemporary societies, cultures and economies are also digitally dependent. It is no longer possible, for example, to contemplate a school, hospital or business fully functioning for more than a few days without its digital management systems or digital communications.

So, how has this state of digital dependency come about? The scale and scope of everything just described owes much to the IT industry and, in particular, what is termed 'Big Tech' – the large multinational tech corporations that oversee the core infrastructure that underpins our digitized lives. Together, these corporations have become 'defining institutions of our day' (Birch and Bronson 2022), modern-day equivalents of Big Oil, Big Banking, Big Tobacco and other twentieth-century power blocs. The likes of Amazon, Microsoft, Meta, Alphabet, TenCent and Alibaba now wield disproportionate influence over the development and take-up of digital services. This gatekeeping role is evident in how Big Tech dominates the digitization of public services such as education, health and welfare, as well as economic sectors such as finance and retail. Any significant development – societal, cultural or economic – is now likely to involve one (or more) of these familiar IT industry names in one way or another.

At the same time, it is also important to remind ourselves how everything just described takes place through planetary-scale physical infrastructure. While the IT industry works hard to promote the illusion that its products and services are somehow virtual, immaterial and 'in the cloud', the reality is far more concrete and dirtier (Taffel 2025). All the digitizations just described are reliant on sprawling material infrastructures and convoluted supply chains. For example, it was reckoned that over a billion smartphones and around 400 million personal computing devices were manufactured in 2024 (Statista 2024). All these devices are assembled from components made from rare minerals and metals (such as lithium and coltan) that originate in places such as Congo and Brazil. Most of these devices are assembled in countries such as Vietnam, China and India, and then shipped many times around the world. While mostly sold to consumers in richer parts of the world, these laptops, smartphones and other devices are a truly global concern.

This planetary digital infrastructure does not stop at the point of sale. Once purchased, these devices are then connected through 1.4 million kilometres of undersea copper and optical fibre cabling sunk beneath the world's oceans to carry transcontinental internet traffic. While we are encouraged to think of digital bits and bytes as ephemeral, much of the world's data is processed and stored in over 100,000 data centres scattered around the planet, the biggest of which each contain upwards of 5,000 computer servers. Elsewhere, as these digital devices begin to age and fall out of fashion, a multibillion dollar 'e-waste' industry dumps discarded hardware into landfill sites in the poorest corners of Ghana, Nigeria, Pakistan, India, China and Brazil. The cumulative impact of all these operations is hard to understate – continually expanding as global demand for digital products and services increases year-by-year.

How digital technology became too big to ignore

These machinations tend to be glossed over in conversations around digital technology, primarily because they simply feel too vast to properly contemplate. However, the true nature of the digital ecosystem is occasionally laid bare through various breakdowns and glitches. These include isolated public outcries over the ethics of digital supply chains – exposés of draconian working conditions in Shenzhen factories which contrast awkwardly with the luxury retail prices attached to the products that these factory workers are assembling. Similarly, sporadic reports will detail how the development of AI systems depends on swathes of precariously employed, low-paid 'ghost labour' that steps in when the technology cannot recognize things – taking responsibility for content moderation, data labelling, language translation and so on (Casilli 2024). This was illustrated in outcries over Kenyan content moderators being paid less than $2 an hour to filter out traumatic material as part of the initial development of the Chat GPT generative AI tool.

While such stories highlight the shocking dependence of the IT industry on worker exploitation in some of the poorest parts of the world, public consciousness in Western countries tends to respond to concerns that are closer to home. The 2013 Edward Snowden revelations were an early wake-up call – alerting US citizens to relentless state and commercial surveillance of their technology use. Since then, public concerns have been triggered by high-profile panics around online disinformation campaigns and commercial data breaches. Alongside this, many people have also tired of the relentless hype around obviously egregious developments such as cryptocurrencies, non-fungible tokens (NFTs) and Mark Zuckerberg's ill-fated 'Metaverse'. We have also seen protests against ethically dubious state rollouts of technology such as facial recognition and lethal autonomous weapons. If one takes the time to look, there are plenty of bad news stories now circulating around digital technology.

All this is fuelling public distrust around digital technology. At the beginning of the 2010s, *The Economist* magazine picked up on what they termed 'the coming tech-lash' (Woodridge 2013). Throughout the 2000s, it was reasoned, general publics had remained relatively upbeat about the convenience of online shopping, social media and the democratic potential of the online 'global village'. At this point, purchasing a new smartphone was still considered to be an exciting moment in one's life. Yet, by the start of the 2010s, this digital optimism began to run out of steam. Indeed, some sort of tech-lash certainly seems to have gained momentum over the past few years. The beginning of the 2020s saw public trust in companies such as Meta and Google hit all-time lows (Washington Post 2021), while Elon Musk, Jeff Bezos and other tech titans continue to be treated with suspicion and contempt. For many people, then, the digital hopes and dreams of the 2000s have gone distinctly sour. As Sharon Vallor (2022) puts it: 'We used to get excited about technology – what happened?'

How digital technology became too big to criticize

Considering everything just outlined, it might seem reasonable to anticipate this growing popular critical consciousness around digital technology to be prompting waves of mass public dissent and demand for change. Yet, the steadily rising sales figures and stock prices of major tech corporations suggest otherwise. Even if populations around the world are becoming disenchanted with the digital age, they continue to consume digital technology at ever increasing rates. The tech-lash seems to have been followed by little more than grudging acceptance amongst tech-using publics that there is little that can be done when it comes to improving the digital experience.

Such passivity reflects how general populations have been conditioned to respond to digital technology. First, is the commonplace way (often referred to as technological determinism) that technology is presented by policymakers and industry as an autonomous force that drives social progress and determines the nature of society. Whatever we do, there is no option to stop the development of new technologies – from the internet to AI – from having an inevitable impact on our lives. This sense of powerlessness is reinforced (and made acceptable) by the residual hope that these new technologies exist to make our lives better. There seems to be a hard-wired response to new digital innovations as inherently beneficial – something that might save time, reduce effort, be more precise and/or function at vastly increased scales and speeds. This optimism often tips over into what Evgeny Morozov (2013) and others have termed 'techno-solutionism' – the expectation that digital technologies offer potential correctives, solutions and 'fixes' to societal problems. All this results in endless cycles of hype, hope and disappointment. While many people's lives have been blighted by previous digital failures and letdowns, it is very hard to let go of the hope that the *next* digital technology will somehow be different.

Anyone attempting to fight against this perpetual cycle of digital expansion clearly faces an uphill struggle. If nothing else, the IT industry works very hard to ensure that we do not pay too much attention to the digital technologies in our lives. Considerable efforts are made to distract consumers with a constant churn of new versions and product upgrades. Even if we stop to question the digital technologies that we are using, it is almost impossible to scrutinize them properly. Our devices come in impenetrable tightly sealed cases, while the coding of software and apps is similarly 'black-boxed' and shut off from inspection. If a smartphone or laptop 'decides' that a software update is due or that a battery cannot recharge, then there is very little that someone wanting to use that device can do about it. Even the most critically minded technology consumer has very little genuine insight into or control over the digital technologies in their lives. At best, we are expected to be grateful for the veneer of choice that comes with picking the colour of a new smartphone or opting to purchase a Mac rather than PC.

All of this fosters a weary acceptance that digital products and services are above being questioned, challenged and effectively pushed back against. Indeed, we are conditioned to believe that digital technologies are something that we cannot live without. Anyone wanting to keep in touch with extended family and friends is likely to feel beholden to their social media accounts. Anyone opting to stop using a smartphone altogether will quickly

The Need for Digital Change 7

find it more difficult to continue with their daily routines. In this sense, owning a smartphone or using social media is not simply an individual lifestyle choice. Instead, excessive consumption of digital technologies is something that has been engineered across many of the key domains of everyday life. This all leads to what various commentators have identified as a default sense of digital 'resignation', where people are led to begrudgingly accept that they have limited opportunities to negotiate how they engage with digital technologies. When it comes to using digital technology in the 2020s, we are firmly conditioned to believe that 'there is no alternative'.

Calling out the harms of digital technology

While it might seem an impossible task, we clearly need to work out ways of moving beyond this uneasy state of digital resignation. Put bluntly, the planet is reaching a tipping point where the downsides of the digital age are beginning to outstrip the benefits. As this chapter will go on to detail, the state of digital excess that now pervades much of the (over)developed world is simply not sustainable. Instead, we need to start thinking in radically different ways about what specific forms of digital technology we want to see in our societies, and what other forms of digital technology might be deemed undesirable, if not utterly unacceptable. This requires us to start making connections between our digital ecosystems and the broader societal and planetary crises that increasingly define these current times. It also requires us to start making connections between the alternative ways of living that we might desire, and different forms of digital technology that might support such change. Digital technology is fully implicated in the societal and environmental problems that the world now faces. How we collectively engage with digital technology over the next few years will be a key determinant of what longer-term futures we can look forward to.

All of this requires approaching the question of digital technology in radically different ways than is currently the norm. This involves seeing the present digital condition as finite rather than endless, and being ready to imagine what comes *after* this current phase of digital excess. We need to believe that digital technology is something that can be contested, challenged and resisted. We

8 Digital Degrowth

need to be open to the idea that different forms of digital technology are possible, and that other forms of digital technology might well be preferable. All this starts with being prepared to call out the specific harms arising from the excessive digitization that we are currently living with.

Digital technology is societally unsustainable

One major reason to begin thinking in radically different ways is the ongoing harms that digital technologies are causing to our societies. Most obvious are the various ways in which digital technologies have come to drive social inequalities and divisions. This stands in direct contradiction to the popular assumption throughout the 1990s and 2000s that computers and the internet would be an inherently democratizing presence in our lives. Instead of something that inevitably increases opportunities for everyone, it is becoming obvious that digital technologies exacerbate and entrench many of the major social fault lines in contemporary society. For this reason alone, it makes little sense to continue supporting the current digital status quo.

These are not particularly novel complaints. Indeed, the term 'digital divide' was coined during the 1990s to describe how access to personal computers and the internet had quickly become patterned along familiar divisions of social class, race, ethnicity, dis/ability and gender. Nearly forty years later, basic access to digital devices, connectivity, bandwidth and other digital infrastructure continues to be as unequally distributed as ever. The 2.6 billion people in the world still lacking internet access are generally living in the most impoverished and marginalized parts of the world. Thereafter, people's capacity to benefit from having access to digital technology follows similar unequal patterns. The 'Matthew Effect' phenomenon of digital opportunities being of most benefit to the already privileged is evident across most applications of digital technology. In short, we are living in a world where digital 'opportunities' and 'conveniences' tend to advantage those who are already most advantaged.

All this means that bold promises of digital transformation are most likely to result in increased social inequalities and exclusions. Think of how the gig economy has panned out to be little more than 'servitude-by-app' – thousands of platforms that allow middle-class people to remotely task working-class people to do things for them. Alternatively, think of the difficulty of carrying out daily life tasks without a smartphone, online banking and/ or reliable connectivity. Of course, large numbers of people do survive without these basic digital resources, but at an increasing cost and marginalization. While any digital inequalities tended to be brushed off by tech enthusiasts during the 1990s and 2000s as a passing phase (with tech apologists often parroting William Gibson's observation that 'the future is here, it just isn't evenly distributed yet'), decades later it now seems obvious that any benefits and advantages that accrue from digital technologies are never going to be distributed evenly. The question is whether those parts of the population that have benefited from having a surfeit of digital technologies in their lives care enough to do anything for those who have not.

Alongside persistent digital inequalities are the worrying ways in which digital technologies are driving various social harms and social injustices. Most recently, these harms have been an invidious part of the recent rise of artificial intelligence into mainstream society. This is evident in reports of AI-driven hiring systems that favour job applicants who most closely match the skewed demographics of employees previously hired by human recruiters (e.g. white, male, college-educated). It is also evident in reports of facial recognition systems that fail to detect people of colour, or voice recognition software that fails to detect particular accents and dialects. Put bluntly, it is fast becoming apparent that setting AI technologies loose in social contexts that are already discriminatory and disadvantaging for minoritized groups simply results in making these social contexts even more discriminatory and disadvantaging.

In short, everyone lucky enough to be not experiencing such disadvantages needs to ask themselves if they are content to live in times when digital technologies and digital systems work to reinforce and amplify existing social divisions in society. So far, it is telling that the problems and concerns just outlined have tended to be raised by activists, researchers and tech-insiders from minority groups and marginalized backgrounds. Indeed, anyone who is black, queer, female and/or ageing is likely to have learnt to not expect new digital technologies to work in their best interests. As Ruha Benjamin (2019) points out, any form of digital (dis)advantage is relational. The flipside of *some* people being empowered and advantaged by digital technologies is that *others* are being disempowered and disadvantaged.

Yet even the most digitally advantaged sectors of society are beginning to increasingly feel that digital technologies are not a wholly positive phenomenon. The past few years have seen rising concerns that digitization is leading to diminished and downgraded ways of doing things. Cory Doctorow (2024) describes this as the 'enshittification' of the digital, a term intended to describe the tendency of established digital platforms and systems to now be decaying in ways that drive the steady degradation of key services and overall living conditions. According to Doctorow, this is an inevitable by-product of the prevailing Silicon Valley business model of: (i) first developing apparently 'free' services to draw in huge numbers of users, then (ii) establishing economies of scale, and finally (iii) steadily monetizing and extracting value from these platforms to claw back value until the original essence of whatever made the service attractive to people has been hollowed out.

Enshittification certainly seems an apt description of people's recent experiences of interacting through a technology such as Facebook, joylessly watching the platform descend into an ever more frustrating means of keeping in touch with family, friends and community. This feeling will also be familiar to anyone who has tried to interact with their local restaurant or municipal services department through a customer service app, or regularly engage with online retail platforms, review sites and news websites. In all these instances, initial promises of digital convenience, flexibility and accessibility have been undone by the subsequent deterioration of core activities and services that the technology is supposed to enhance. Doctorow suggests that tech firms have been able to get away with this through a fundamental lack of regulation and competition, coupled with a stifling of employee power and an underlying public sense of powerlessness to do anything differently (i.e. to switch platforms, install ad-blockers, or simply stop using our devices). All told, the contemporary enclosed and enshittified digital landscape certainly feels a world away from Tim Berners-Lee's utopian ambitions that 'the goal of the web is to serve humanity' (Berners-Lee 2010). Four decades on from the birth of the worldwide web, we are living in a very different (and distinctly dysfunctional) digital environment.

The Need for Digital Change

Digital technology is environmentally unsustainable

Unfortunately, this societal ruinification is only half the story. It is also necessary to face up to the various ways that the ongoing digitization of society is proving to be profoundly environmentally damaging in terms of resource depletion, energy consumption and toxic waste. While complaints over digital divides, algorithmic discrimination and enshittification might feel instantly familiar, we tend to hear far less about the environmental consequences of digital technology. These are problems that might seem more abstract but are no less significant.

One fundamental point of concern is how the manufacturing of digital hardware depends on the extraction of fast-depleting scarce resources – what Toby Miller (2015) describes as the 'dirty material origins and processes' of the digital age. All our digital devices, batteries and attendant infrastructures are assembled from dozens of different non-renewable natural resources, including scarce metals and rare earth elements. Alongside these material origins, the production of digital hardware takes place through a 'vast planetary network' (Crawford and Joler 2018) that facilitates the smelting, processing and mixing of raw materials which are then shipped halfway around the world to be assembled. Each of these stages involves the production (and disposal) of further toxic waste. As Samir Bhowmik (2019) notes, most consumers have no understanding and/or interest in the 'messy' and 'primitive' ways in which their digital devices come into being. There is nothing virtual, artificial or other-worldly about digital technology.

With literally billions of digital devices being manufactured each year, this all comes at a considerable environmental cost. Many of the component materials essential to the manufacture of laptops, smartphones and other devices are in scarce supply. For example, almost half the world's extraction of rare earth elements such as cerium, neodymium and dysprosium (materials used for hard-disc drives, LCD screens and fibre optics) takes place within a 15 km by 19 km area in Inner Mongolia – a location whose resources are non-renewable and fast depleting. The extraction and production of many of these resources is itself environmentally harmful. Much of the mining of rare earth and metals involves the excessive use of chemicals and water, and has led to illegal mining, pollution and deforestation. All of this extraction and environmental exploitation takes place on a grand scale. When the resource implications of this manufacturing process are factored in, conservative estimates suggest that producing one desktop computer expends 240 kilograms of fossil fuels, 22 kilograms of chemicals, and 1,500 kilograms of water (Ensmenger 2018).

Moreover, the ongoing extraction of these metals and minerals is bound up in the geopolitics of some of the poorest and most conflict-disrupted regions in the world. For example, much of the world's coltan supply originates within the Democratic Republic of the Congo, Rwanda and Nigeria – parts of the world where mining industries continue to be denounced for diminished worker rights, unsafe working conditions, forced and child labour. All told, the ever-expanding rates of production of digital devices come at huge environmental and ethical costs. As Maxwell and Miller (2020) conclude, 'consumer electronics and other digital technologies are made in ways that cause some of the worst environmental disasters of our time'.

The environmental harms of digital technology do not stop at the production stage. A second point of concern is the excessive resource implications of emerging technologies such as AI that depend on mass data processing and storage. The data storage industry is built upon a sprawling infrastructure of more than 100,000 physical data centres that are scattered around the world – vast metal and glass warehouses that each require massive amounts of power to function. These data centres occupy large tracts of land, depend on constant air conditioning and cooling, and emit relentless levels of noise. They also require huge amounts of water to keep cool. For example, one study reckons Google's data operations to have used nearly 16 billion litres of water over a twelve-month period (Mytton 2021). Microsoft's entry into AI development through its partnership with OpenAI is reported to have caused the corporation's global water consumption to increase 34 per cent from the previous year, reaching a figure just short of 1.7 billion gallons. This fast-rising consumption is now prompting local governments with data centres within their boundaries to draw up contingency plans to minimize the future impact on residential water supplies (O'Brien and Fingerhut 2023).

Yet perhaps the main Achilles' heel of the data centre industry is its 'the obscene energy demands' (Kolbert 2024). The Irish statistical agency reported in 2022 that the country's seventy data centres were responsible for consuming 14 per cent of the national electricity output. In China, nearly three-quarters of the power consumed by the country's data centres is drawn from coal. Regardless of where in the world they are located, actual data storage operations might account for as little as 6 per cent of a data centre's power consumption, with the vast majority used for back-up systems, 'fail-safe' generators and servers – all secondary parts of the system that only are useful in the event of a breakdown. All told, it is reckoned that the IT and data processing industry already has a greater carbon footprint than the airline industry. Even more worryingly, it is feared that these levels of energy consumption might increase sixfold over the next ten years (BBC News 2024).

If these environmental burdens were not enough, another point of concern is the waste and pollution incurred in dismantling and disposing of digital devices and other hardware once they have outlived their usefulness. The growing problem of e-waste resulting from discarded digital hardware has long been highlighted by environmentalists, with the dumping of devices leading to heightened levels of pollution, contamination and toxic waste in some of the poorest regions of the world. It is estimated that more than 53 million metric tonnes of e-waste are generated each year, with only 17.4 per cent being recycled. Indeed, relatively few raw materials can be salvaged when recycling a digital device, with plastic, glass, aluminium and copper only making up around one-fifth of a smartphone or tablet. Some of the remaining materials are highly toxic and can contain radioactive elements that take millennia to decay. To make matters worse, the toxicity of e-waste is increasing as silicon chips become ever smaller and densely engineered (Kneese 2023).

All told, it seems clear that the rising levels of digital technology production and consumption over the past twenty years is directly implicated in the planetary breakdowns and ecological degradations that we now increasingly experience. Much of this has been exacerbated by an IT industry culture that has come to presume an abundance of resourcing and to privilege efficiency, speed and scale over all other considerations. This has led to an acceptance of convoluted supply chains and wasteful business practices such as 'planned obsolescence' – the deliberate design of digital hardware to slow down after a few years, become incompatible with the latest software, have irreplaceable parts and increasingly short battery life. This has led to an acceptance of software programming that takes up unnecessary amounts of memory (what is termed 'bloatware') and other high bandwidth practices such as streaming that depend on energy-consuming centralized network processing and data storage.

As such, some critics are now beginning to push for serious consideration of the ways in which 'the digital world is costing the earth' (Pitron 2023). It is, of course, difficult to precisely calculate the cumulative environmental burdens implicit in the continued production and consumption of digital technology, with any direct figures remaining 'closely guarded corporate secrets' (Crawford 2024: 693). Nevertheless, it has been reckoned that each stage in the development of a standard deep learning model now results in a carbon footprint equivalent to one month's emissions for the New York City region. Elsewhere, getting into a 'conversation' of a few dozen prompts with ChatGPT has been estimated to consume half a litre of water (Li et al. 2023). Similarly, using ChatGPT to search for information is reckoned to expend up to five times the energy of finding the same information with a conventional search engine (Crawford 2024). While these figures might not appear much in isolation, they soon mount up through the billions of times a month that services such as Chat GPT and Google are used. All told, it is becoming clear that such environmental costs cannot continue indefinitely. As Wim Vanderbauwhede (2021) concedes: "By 2040 emissions from computing alone will be more than half the emissions level acceptable to keep global warming below 1.5°C. This growth in computing emissions is unsustainable: it would make it virtually impossible to meet the emissions warming limit."

Pushing back against digital growth

It is perhaps understandable that very few of the concerns just outlined tend to get picked up in mainstream discussions about the digital age and digital innovation. From a commercial point of view digital divides and e-waste are not talking points that are likely to motivate consumers to rush out and upgrade their smartphones. Even those who do not stand to profit from the sale of digital products may also consider it largely pointless to dwell

The Need for Digital Change   15

for too long on such issues. Even the most well-intentioned individual is unable to do much in response to hearing how computer use contributes to climate collapse. Yet, everything that has just been outlined needs to be taken seriously as grounds for challenging the current forms of digitization that dominate our lives. This is not to argue for completely giving up on all things digital. Instead, all the contentions just raised relate to the particularly excessive and capricious modes of digital technology that have come to the fore over the past ten years or so. One of the key lines of argument underpinning this book is that digital technology does not have to be like this. Other forms of digital technology are certainly possible.

All of this points to the need to understand digital technology as a lot more than just devices and software. Instead, it is important to pay close attention to the social, economic, political, cultural and historical conditions within which digital technologies are developed, produced and used. Seen from a 'sociotechnical' perspective, then, any digital device, algorithm or data centre is part of a complex system of technical designs, scientific laws, physical environments, natural resources, economic principles, legal and regulatory forms, political forces, organizational bureaucracy, human labour, social conventions and practices (Hughes 1983). Any effort to reimagine digital technology therefore needs to engage with all these aspects. For example, close attention needs to be paid to the manufacturing of digital technology – complex supply chains, raw materials, exploitative labour, patents systems and industry standards. It is also important to pay close attention to the political economy of digital technology – tech corporations, government policies, finance systems, stock markets and circuits of investment. All told, there are many different factors behind the digital technologies that have come to dominate our societies. This raises important questions around how the parameters of digital development are set by particular social expectations, political priorities, economic interests and popular visions of the future.

Above all, this raises the importance of engaging with the politics of digital technology. As Langdon Winner (1980) pointed out, on the one hand this relates to how technological artefacts are designed and implemented (often unconsciously) in ways that have particular societal effects. Here, Winner gave the example of the mechanical tomato harvester in the 1940s, an innovation that

16   Digital Degrowth

fulfilled an economic promise to increase productivity and lower farming costs, but also steadily restricted tomato growing to large farms while prompting the cultivation of less-tasty tomatoes. On the other hand, we also need to consider the ways that technological artefacts are reinforced by (and, in turn, reinforce) specific social conditions and political arrangements. Here, Winner gave the example of nuclear power stations, a technology that he considered most compatible with centralized authoritarian states with comprehensive security capabilities. As Jane Bennett reiterated, 'it is hard to imagine locally-run, democratically organized reactors' (1987: 662).

As well as helping make sense of why we have the dominant forms of digital technology that we do, this view of the politics of technology also prompts us to think through how things might be otherwise. While dominant technologies usually work to enforce dominant power dynamics and interests, engaging with the politics of technology raises the possibility of thinking how other values, interests and agendas might be baked into the design and development of digital technologies. What forms of agricultural technology might support small farms to produce tastier tomatoes? What forms of energy technology might be an appropriate part of locally run and democratically organized societies? What forms of digital technology might work to replenish the natural environment and enhance the social well-being of those who use them?

Digital technology and the imperative of growth

In working out how to start rethinking an alternative politics of digital technology, it is worth reflecting on what has led to the forms of digital excess that we currently endure. One inescapable factor is the ways in which the development of digital technology over the past few decades has been built fundamentally around ideas of growth. Presumptions of growth run deep within the commercial ambitions of the IT sector, as well as the ways in which digital innovation is seen by policymakers and business leaders as an essential driver of economic growth. Indeed, digital technology development is firmly wedded to a 'linear' notion of growth-driven innovation, where 'investment in science yields technological innovation, which delivers economic growth, which in turn leads to job creation, welfare and prosperity –

including (technological) solutions to environmental problems' (Kerschner et al. 2018: 1620). In addition, growth is also a key part of the conceptual foundations of academic computer science and the practical motivations of software designers. Even amongst the general public, digital technology is understood as a means of doing more things, more effectively and more expansively. One does not turn to digital technologies to do things in more restrained, modest or reduced ways.

Before we can begin imagining any alternatives, it is worth unpacking the ways in which growth has become baked into our shared understandings of what digital technology is. For example, a defining feature of IT industry thinking is an obsession with 'scalability' and a 'scale first, profit later' approach – the ambition to move beyond localized actions and engage in universalized actions that can reach new users and new regions, and therefore dominate markets on a worldwide basis. This ties in with tech industry beliefs in 'network effects', where online services and systems with the largest reach and biggest user bases are understood to generate the greatest gains in value and utility. Similarly, from a technical point of view, modern technology development is driven by ambitions of engineering ever greater processing power and high-performance computing – maximizing levels of throughput, bandwidth and data compression speeds, striving for faster response times and greater storage capacity. All of this leads to the pursuit of 'optimization' coupled with an acceptance of rapid rates of 'churn' and obsolescence, accompanied by the common goal of improving upon and superseding every new innovation.

This pursuit of expansion, growth and 'doing more' is endemic to the digital technology sector – underpinning core business strategies and IT industry ambitions to achieve global impacts through 'thinking big' and 'moving fast'. This is certainly evident in how tech industry actors have talked about themselves over the past thirty years. For example, Microsoft's corporate strapline during the mid-2010s was the immodest ambition to 'empower every person and every organization on the planet to achieve more'. Such mission statements combine corporate hubris with genuine ambition to operate at the largest scales possible. Similar principles are also enshrined in some of the fundamental rules-of-thumb passed down amongst software engineers and computer scientists, with received wisdoms such as Moore's Law, Koomey's

18 Digital Degrowth

Law and Kryder's Law all laying down self-fulfilling rules for how digital technology development becomes faster, denser, more powerful and efficient as each year passes. Crucially, this fundamental orientation toward growth underpins how future forms of digital technology are imagined and approached. As Daniel Pargman (2015) puts it, the direction of travel within IT industry and tech development circles is only ever conceived in terms of 'more' tech, 'better' tech and 'faster' tech.

Digital technology and the capitalist imperative

Of course, none of this is merely the pursuit of growth-for-growth's-sake. Instead, the tech sector's embrace of digital growth is entwined with the economic interests of capital and the logics of capitalism (Sadowski 2025). In an obvious sense, the current dominant forms of excessive digitization that have been the focus of this chapter are aggressively commercial in character – built around hyper-competitive marketplaces for the sale of devices, software and services, attracting all manner of corporations and companies competing to maximize market share and stock prices. Tellingly, most tech companies are not striving to be profitable per se, but are following a business model of chasing repeated rounds of venture capital, start-up financing and angel investment, which in turn is seen to require ever-increasing market valuations and unrealistic promises of vastly inflated returns on investment. This all results in digital technology that is imbued with economizing logics of efficiency, cost-effectiveness, economic growth, market expansion and other characteristics of contemporary capitalism.

The capitalist imperative is also evident in the inherently exploitative character of current digital technology. Take, for example, how digital technology has become a key means through which most facets of public life are now appropriated for profit – what might be seen in Marxian terms as 'primitive accumulation'. Indeed, one of the main business models of contemporary digital technology is profiting from the extraction of people's data. In addition are the ways in which digital technology is now entwined with what Nancy Fraser (2022) describes as the logics of capitalism as a societal order. One example of this is how digital technologies are designed to prey on extra-economic supports to function. This can be seen in the ways in

The Need for Digital Change   *19*

which digital technologies are designed to free ride on unpaid work to amass economic value. Another manifestation of this logic is how digital technology manufacturing depends on the exploitation of natural resources to amass economic value. While the IT industry is keen to promote itself in ultra-modern, other-worldly terms, digital products and services are clearly dependent upon the exploitation of what Jason Moore (2021) calls 'cheap nature'.

In all these ways, we are now faced with a dominant form of digital technology that personifies the exploitative, rapacious nature of contemporary capitalism. This raises the troubling question of where things are likely to progress if allowed to continue unchecked. At present, there is every reason to expect digital capitalism to become even more rapacious – devouring even more natural resources, sucking up more free labour, further hollowing-out our public sectors and communities. Indeed, endless extractive expansionism is an explicit feature of how the tech industry sees itself. As Fieke Jansen puts it:

> These developments need to be placed against a backdrop of infinite growth, scalability, resource, and data extraction of internet infrastructures ... The operation, maintenance, and expansion of the internet infrastructures needed to accommodate this growth will involve further environmental harm. (2023: 60)

Digital technology and the military imperative

Looking back on the history of the tech industry since the 1950s, a further significant influence on the pernicious character of digital excess that we have today has been the close involvement of the US military-industrial complex in commissioning and funding the development of various areas of digital innovation. Indeed, many key developments in Silicon Valley during the Cold War period of the 1950s to 1990s were bankrolled by US military and intelligence agency contracts and grants. One well-publicized example of this was the Defense Department-funded ARPANET project in the late 1960s that established the first iteration of the internet. Yet, military funding has underpinned many other areas of everyday computing, from early support in the 1950s for semiconductor research through to defence and intelligence agency funding of the initial development of Google. Even after the end of the Cold War, the US Defense Advanced Research

20 Digital Degrowth

Projects Agency has continued to support the initial development of various technologies with military purposes in mind, from autonomous cars to the technology behind the Siri iPhone app (Weinberger 2017).

These industrial military origins have undoubtedly shaped the nature and character of today's digital technology. For example, the current logic of the internet reflects ARPANET's design as a decentralized computer network capable of functioning in the event of nuclear conflict. It might be argued that Google's business model of monetizing surveillance of its users reflects its initial funding by the CIA and NSA. In this sense, much of what Silicon Valley has done over the past fifty years or so reflects 'the imperatives of a deeply militarized society' (Gonzalez 2024). It is no coincidence that we now have an IT industry with expansionist, all-conquering and deeply invasive ambitions that regularly tip over into immoral and pathological corporate behaviours (Brueckner 2013). It is no coincidence that today's digital technologies are well-suited to monitoring, controlling, policing and oppressing entire populations, and that Silicon Valley can be seen as a key extension of US imperialism (Kwet 2024). As Gonzalez (2024) concludes, the internet might have been considerably different if the development of ARPANET had been funded by a civilian agency such as the US Department of Education. Similarly, we might have had a much less wasteful model of computing manufacture if the development of semiconductors had been funded by the US Department of Energy. As it is, however, we are left with technologies originating from very different militaristic values and priorities.

This all sets up a key challenge to take forward into the remainder of this book – just how can digital technology be disentangled from capitalist logics of growth, expansion, excess and extraction? How can the development of digital technology be detached from financial markets and the hollow pursuit of venture capitalist funding and speculative investment? How can digital technology be divested of its reliance on military patronage? Instead, how is it possible for digital technologies to be reimagined as matters of care, collective interest and solidarity? What might smaller-scale, local forms of digital technology look like? While we might have been conditioned to think that there is no alternative, what might post-capitalist, peaceful and ecologically minded forms of digital technology look like, and how might we develop digital technology that is better for people, communities and the planet?

Conclusions

This chapter has set out an initial case for what is wrong with the digital technologies that have come to prominence over the past twenty years or so. In short, we are currently enduring forms of digital technology that are societally and environmentally harmful to the point of becoming unsustainable. These forms of digital technology are excessive, aggressive, expansionist and all-encompassing – driven by an IT industry, financial markets and military patronage that arrogantly presume an endless abundance of digital resourcing and an entitlement to exploit whatever possible in the pursuit of 'innovation' and 'progress'. If we have not already got there, then we are fast approaching the tipping point where these forms of digital technology start to do a lot more harm than good. Having established these points of contention, we now need to consider what we want instead. How can digital tech be part of a realistic liveable future, and what would it take to achieve this?

All this points to the need to reimagine the value and values of digital technology. How can we reframe the value of technology away from capitalist notions of profit, return on investment and stock market standings? Instead, how might the value of digital technology be recognized in terms of helping our communities, societies and environments survive and ideally flourish, contributing to safety, comfort, happiness and other forms of 'lived value' (Mulgan 2013)? Alongside this, how might we ground digital technologies in a new ethical basis of values that are aligned with ambitions of collective well-being, care, mutual solidarity with other people and shared obligation to the planet? This, then, is a driving motivation of the rest of this book – looking to move beyond the current problematic forms of digital excess as outlined in this chapter, toward a meaningful transformative vision of how else we might want to be living with digital technology.

Book overview

These are complex ideas to cover in a relatively short space. As means of orientation the book will now progress as follows:

Chapter 2: Does Tech Have Any Solutions?
We consider the popular belief that social and environmental harms associated with digital technologies can be overcome through even more intensified forms of digital innovation. This chapter considers the obvious limitations of tech industry promises of 'Green Tech' and 'Tech for Social Good'. It concludes that these speculative solutions do little more than give a free pass to the continued expansion of digital capitalism. Instead, far more radical change is required.

Chapter 3: Beginning to Think Differently About Digital Technology
Here we take inspiration from a variety of alternate approaches to thinking differently about more humane, fairer and caring forms of digital technology. Attention is then turned to how degrowth thinking offers a powerful addition to these ongoing movements, adding a much-needed environmental focus to rethinking digital technology along scaled-back and slowed-down lines.

Chapter 4: The Case for Digital Degrowth
This chapter sketches out what a philosophy of digital degrowth might look like – considering existing degrowth discussions of non-digital technologies alongside Ivan Illich's idea of tools for conviviality. The chapter also highlights existing 'degrowth adjacent' thinking that has begun to emerge within the margins of computer science, software development and digital activist communities.

Chapter 5: Finding Alternatives in the Here and Now
This chapter addresses two immediate aspects of practically putting digital degrowth ideas into action: (i) working out ways to *oppose* current forms of digital technology that are clearly irredeemable to human and environmental flourishing; and (ii) working out ways to *support* existing forms of digital technology that are clearly conducive to degrowth ambitions. It offers vari-

ous examples of how alternative post-capitalist forms of digital technology are already being realized at a local, collective level.

Chapter 6: Future Innovations
This chapter considers the longer-term challenge of innovating *new* forms of digital technology that can support radically different social relations and practices, political dynamics and environmental impacts that align with degrowth principles. It covers various areas of emerging thinking and speculative innovation – ranging from salvage computing through to nature-powered and biodegradable computing – that encourage us to think expansively and ambitiously about other forms of digital living.

Chapter 7: Where Now? Everywhere But Here!
Finally, we consider the challenges that face any attempt to realize these ambitions for better digital futures. This chapter discusses how digital degrowth can be advanced as a social movement that is locally determined and aligned with a wider societal decoupling from economic growth and capitalist imperatives. While we should not be naive about the difficulties of any such change, transitioning away from excessive growth-driven digitization now needs to be pushed as a key action point for the mid twenty-first century and beyond.

2

Does Tech Have Any Solutions?

Introduction

Most people working in and around technology tend to be remarkably untroubled by the issues outlined in Chapter 1. Indeed, many tech industry insiders (and their supporters) remain confident that any environmental and societal harms are temporary glitches that will soon be overcome through the development of even more powerful new technologies. According to this logic, the development of 'fair' AI systems will put an end to algorithmic discrimination and other digital harms. Similarly, concerns around carbon emissions will be sidestepped through alternative energy approaches. Such optimism follows the popular solutionist mindset that problems (no matter how big) can be fixed through digital innovation and human ingenuity. For the time being, at least, many experts remain confident that we can continue looking forward to an even greater digital future. Regardless of any of the issues raised in Chapter 1, mainstream opinion remains buoyed by the reassurance that 'tech will save us'.

Such complacency is not unique to the current digital age. Indeed, faith in 'technological fixes' arguably peaked during the 1960s' development of nuclear power, space technology and other innovations of the Cold War period (Johnson 2018). Yet, current generations seem remarkably willing to buy into the specific idea of digital technologies offering ready solutions to the world's major problems. Morgan Ames (2019) attributes this to the 'charismatic' and other-worldly nature of digital technology. In a similar vein, Campolo and Crawford (2020) point to the 'enchanted' ways in which emerging technologies such as AI are perceived; they see this mass enchantment as driven by the common belief that digital technologies 'are both magical and superhuman – beyond what we can understand'. Viewed through this wonderous lens, there is no problem or challenge that cannot be remedied through the development of yet more new technology.

Techno-solutions to the societal unsustainability of digital tech

Techno-solutionist thinking certainly abounds when it comes to the various concerns raised in Chapter 1 around the technological exacerbation of deep-rooted societal harms. Despite digital technology being a long-standing source of social disadvantage and disharmony, there is now increasing talk around the design, development and deployment of new digital technologies to address the biggest impending social problems of our times. This is often expressed through mantras such as 'Tech for Good', 'AI for Good', 'Data for Good' and similar (see Madianou 2021; Aula and Bowles 2023). Of course, definitions of this 'good' tend to remain vague. For example, Alison Powell et al. (2022) define 'Tech for Good' as any 'technology developed or employed to advance human flourishing or for social purpose'. Perhaps because of this catch-all quality, the idea of digital technology 'for good' is now driving various new waves of tech enthusiasm in fields such as education, healthcare, humanitarian aid and other areas of public and civic responsibility.

Most of the Big Tech corporations highlighted in Chapter 1 have added a 'for good' dimension to their ambitions. For example, Google's 'AI for Social Good' group boasts 'a shared focus on positive social impact' and a mission statement of 'Applying AI to make a difference in the lives of those who need it most'. Landmark projects range from the development of AI tools to predict the real-time spread of wildfires, through to apps designed to help otherwise reticent children learn to read. There is growing interest in AI-driven 'homelessness support systems' and predictive modelling that can save endangered species. Such projects are driven by optimistic and solutionist ambitions, where the development of digital technologies inevitably leads on to solving big ticket problems. As is usually the way in Silicon Valley, this work tends to be talked up in grand terms of global transformation and revolution. As Mark Zuckerberg (2012) put it in a letter to Facebook shareholders:

> There is a huge need and a huge opportunity to get everyone in the world connected, to give everyone a voice and to help transform society for the future. The scale of the technology and infrastructure that must be built is unprecedented, and we believe this is the most important problem we can focus on.

At first glance, such claims around emerging technology might be dismissed as empty commercial sloganeering and marketing. The suffix 'for Social Good' certainly provides powerful Big Tech corporations with a means to disingenuously align their commercial interests with humanitarian ideals (Magalhães and Couldry 2021). As Richard Gall (2021) puts it: '"Tech for good" isn't really a movement. It's more of a posture ... a useful phrase that allows users to greenwash an industry that has little interest in anything other than entrenching its own power and wealth.' Yet, while some elements of the tech industry have undoubtedly latched on to 'Tech for Good' in a self-serving manner, many tech firms present themselves as driven by a belief that digital technology is capable of leveraging substantial social change. In this sense, the main problem with the idea of 'Tech for Good' is not outright dishonesty per se, but tech industry naivety and/or hubris about the societal impact that any technology can have. Corporations such as Google and Meta wield great influence, and their confidence in tackling big social issues inevitably has far reaching consequences, regardless of the actual extent to which their technologies can address the problems they purport to solve.

Of course, the capacity of digital technology to actually effect any social change remains a moot point. The past twenty years or so have seen poverty levels soar in even the most prosperous countries, along with forced migration, health inequalities and most other societal ills continuing to reach ever more catastrophic levels. All told, there are very few social issues that appear to have been meaningfully addressed (let alone solved) through the application of digital technology. As such, it objectively makes little sense to expect any new tech efforts to be capable of significantly shifting the needle on the societal concerns outlined in Chapter 1. Instead, we need to push back against the prevailing wisdom that the answer to technology-induced societal problems is somehow the development of additional technology. The driving premise of this book is that we need to think much more innovatively than that.

What is wrong with 'Tech for Good'?

Advocates of Tech for Good might consider these latter comments to be rather mean-spirited and regressive. Any criticisms of Tech for Good are usually rebutted as negativity on the part of non-technologists who have never built technologies and who are incapable of 'thinking outside of the box'. Yet it makes little sense to expect technological innovation to somehow overcome the societal problems raised so far in this book. Indeed, there are various reasons to suspect that putting our collective faith in the Tech for Good approach might only exacerbate levels of societal division, disadvantage and dysfunction. In short, there are very good grounds to argue that Tech for Good is not a desirable way forward.

First and foremost are the narrow redefinitions of what constitutes social problems. The idea of Tech for Good understandably focuses on societal issues to which digital technology is particularly suited, or, worse still, reduces complex social issues to overly simplified forms that digital technology can then get applied to. As Aula and Bowles (2023) put it, the Tech for Good movement tends to narrowly define what constitutes social good 'through the attributes of novel computational techniques'. This means that complicated social issues that are generally accepted to be insurmountable tend to get overlooked, as are issues that are not deemed worthy (or simply interesting) enough to sustain the attention of tech developers. All this runs the risk that Tech for Good efforts are driven by technological – rather than social – motivations and result in the inappropriate deployment of technology.

In addition, Tech for Good efforts tend to frame social issues as best addressed through privatized and corporate efforts (Madianou 2021). As Radhika Radhakrishnan (2021) contends, the application of 'Tech for Social Good' in fields such as healthcare and education are underpinned by presumptions that private sector interventions are the most effective means of redressing shortfalls in public services. Such assumptions distract attention away from the need to direct time and resources toward improving the public sector. In addition, Radhakrishnan argues that Tech for Good interventions in Global South contexts push the importance of investment in capital in the form of digital technology, while devaluing the idea of investing in workforces and improved working conditions.

In all these ways, then, the idea of 'Tech for Good' should not be seen simply as a benign addition to existing efforts to improve society, but as an appeal to fundamentally change the nature of what gets done and who is doing it. In particular, the continued promotion of Tech for Social Good is rooted in narrow understandings of ethics, values and virtue. As Alison Powell and colleagues reason, this is evident in at least three ways. First, in a highly individualized conception of virtue, where 'good' ends are seen to arise from individual entities (such as a tech company or individual software developer) behaving virtuously, rather than 'doing good' being a collective process. Second, in a sense of 'tech exceptionalism', where digital technologies give these individual entities freedom to act virtuously, within social contexts that are otherwise usually experienced by others as heavily bounded and structured. Finally, in a linear 'cause and effect' conception of how societal change comes about (doing X to achieve Y), with digital technology framed as a lever to achieve virtuous outcomes. In all these ways, then, the complexities of societal problems and how to address them are drastically oversimplified.

Indeed, it is also important to acknowledge what is *not* being said within the continued promotion of Tech for Social Good, where there is a tendency to sideline the complex and messy nature of the social contexts that these projects take place within. This is evident in how talk of 'Tech for Social Good' tends to sideline consideration of the actual needs, viewpoints and understandings of the local groups and communities who are having 'good' done to them. Here it might be argued that Tech for Social Good efforts tend to frame social issues in decontextualized ways that sideline the interests and knowledges of the populations they supposedly serve.

All this makes it very difficult to find comfort in a future based around the idea of heightened levels of digital technology production and consumption somehow improving society. These projects are notably limited in terms of what topics are deemed 'good' and worthy, what specific problems are focused on and what outcomes are anticipated (and eventually celebrated). Crucially, these efforts distract us from acknowledging (let alone tackling) issues of structural power and systemic disadvantage. There is also very little interest in projects and initiatives that result in outcomes likely to challenge dominant interests or upset the status quo. All told, if we are serious about addressing the issues of societal sustainability outlined in Chapter 1, there is little to be gained by pinning our hopes on digital technology as the main means of success.

Techno-solutions to the environmental unsustainability of digital tech

In fairness, it is unclear whether the IT industry fully believes that it is possible to overcome societal problems through technology. Despite the hype, the application of Tech for Good to pressing social problems seems to be something of a side-hustle for many tech actors, and certainly not anything that IT firms are keen to be held accountable for. Like most aspects of corporate social responsibility, many Tech for Good efforts are understood (at least implicitly) as aspirational if not largely symbolic. Instead, if tech industry actors do have genuine faith in the power of technology solutions, then this seems to be in relation to addressing problems of environmental sustainability. This is evident in strong beliefs that digital technologies can be designed, developed and deployed to offer a ready way out of our current environmental woes, and perhaps even enhance future environmental sustainability. With corporations such as Google proudly proclaiming their commitment to 'building a carbon-free future for all', perhaps there is far less for us to worry about in terms of environmental breakdown and climate collapse than might be imagined?

Tech industry ambitions around addressing environmental

problems are driven by two parallel lines of thinking. First is the idea that the development of even more sophisticated forms of digital technology might help combat the effects of climate collapse and offer our best hope of surviving a climate constrained future. Indeed, while the capitalist classes spent much of the 2010s aggressively downplaying (or outright denying) climate change, the 2020s have seen a similarly aggressive push for climate solutionism. This is the notion of innovating and investing our way out of the climate crisis, through new technology and a refashioned 'climate capitalism'. This can-do attitude is captured in recent bestselling books with subtitles such as 'Winning the race to zero emissions and solving the crisis of our age' (Rathi 2024) and 'How we can be the first generation to build a sustainable planet' (Richie 2024). Such visions of harnessing digital technology to address climate problems are grandly referred to as an alliance of 'Green & Blue'; in other words:

> A new marriage between the Green of our habitats – natural, synthetic and artificial, from the biosphere to the infosphere, from urban environments to economic, social, and political circumstances – and the Blue of our digital technologies, from mobile phones to social platforms, from the Internet of Things to Big Data, from AI to future quantum computing. (Floridi and Nobre 2020)

The potential of 'Green & Blue' innovation is presented as being almost limitless. One prominent area of interest involves harnessing AI technology as a means of combatting climate collapse. As Microsoft's 'AI for Earth' mission statement put it, this is the vision of 'helping save the planet with data science'. One recent focus for such work has been the development of AI models to predict fast-changing climate and weather patterns, identifying changes in global temperatures and areas at risk of flooding, extreme heat and winds. In addition, there are AI-driven efforts to support the conservation and management of ecosystems, tackling everything from illegal poaching to deforestation and reef erosion. Another key area of development is the application of AI tools to enable the reduction of emissions amongst high-polluting industries. In this spirit, Boston Consulting Group's (2023) 'How AI Can Speed Climate Action' report reckoned that AI-driven systems could mitigate up to 10 per cent of global greenhouse gas emissions by 2030. All told, the tech industry and its enablers are pushing hard for government support and public funding for such ventures. As a joint report from Microsoft and PwC warned: 'there is a huge opportunity forgone if leaders and decision-makers do not help enable AI innovations for the environment' (Microsoft/PwC 2019: 9).

These proposed solutions run alongside hopes that the tech industry itself can transition to environmentally friendly ways of operating. All these shifts in corporate strategy anticipate a new phase of digital technology use and growth supported by IT industry efforts to make greater use of renewable energy, BECCS (bioenergy with carbon capture and storage) and other forms of decarbonized energy. In this spirit, the beginning of the 2020s saw many Big Tech corporations make bold pledges and commitments to tackle climate change and become 'net zero' or even 'net negative'. Amazon's Climate Pledge promised to reach net zero by 2040, with Jeff Bezos highlighting this move as essential to averting the 'biggest threat to our planet'. Similarly, Apple committed to all its products and supply chains being carbon neutral by 2030, pledging to 'make products using only recycled or renewable materials – so we prioritise, responsibly source and recover materials'. As Apple's marketing boasts, 'Because the earth won't wait. Neither will we.'

Another focus has been the promise to establish green forms of data centres and clean up the environmental impact of the data storage industry. This has seen grand pledges to move data centres away from 'dirty' electricity sources, to become 'water positive' and be constructed using environmentally friendly materials. One consortium of European data centre companies launched a 'Climate Neutral Data Centre Pact', with a headline commitment to their facilities becoming 'climate neutral' by 2050. Tellingly, some of these sustainable innovation efforts are now exploring how the natural world might be enrolled into such solutions. One indicative example is the burgeoning interest in setting up data centres under the seas and oceans. Microsoft has been experimenting with this approach through its Project Natick – sinking small 12-metre-long prototype data centres with over 850 servers onto the seabed off California and the Scottish islands. In 2023, the Chinese Hainan Undersea Data Centre Project sunk over 100 modules off Hainan island, comprising over 60,000 computers intended to remain *in situ* for up to twenty-five years and save 122 million kilowatt-hours of electricity each year in comparison to similar land-based data centres.

Questioning the promise of 'Green Tech'

All these IT industry efforts frame the digital future in undeniably appealing ways – anticipating a new era of 'green growth' characterized by continued expansive use of digital technologies without the current adverse environmental impacts. In one sense, the promise of doing anything to act against the threat of climate change is welcome. Indeed, such thinking is certainly preferable to tech corporations ignoring sustainability and environmental issues altogether. As Kate Soper suggests, 'optimists who seek rescue in technology' are less dangerous than the alternate nihilist view that one sometimes finds in tech communities, i.e. 'Carpe diem fatalists who think it is too late to salvage the planet, so we should enjoy it while we can' (Soper 2023: 107).

Yet, it is naive to see these Green Tech efforts as motivated solely by environmental or altruistic concerns. Instead, the underpinning logic at play here is that developing environmentally sustainable forms of digital technology makes good business sense. For example, marketing for the undersea data centre firm 'Subsea Cloud' boasts various telling commercial rationales for undersea data storage and processing. As well as reducing data storage costs by up to 90 per cent, one of Subsea's main selling points is that undersea data centres can be located close to major coastal metropolitan markets – 'we are infinitely scalable near densely populated areas'. Whereas the capacity for the data centre industry to build on land is both expensive and limited, 'the seafloor is virtually unlimited in its capacity to safely house our data centres'. Importantly, the ability to quickly establish offshore data centres allows firms to meet government requirements for data to be stored locally within national boundaries.

Beyond the economic growth motive there are various other causes for concern around the tech industry's recent interest in the environment. For example, some experts point to the 'rebound effect' risk that new green technologies will end up further enmeshing consumers and producers within complex supply chains of excessive consumption and production that cause further environmental problems. This relates to what is known as 'Jevons Paradox' – the logical incentive under capitalism for growth-driven firms to use any efficiencies they make to increase levels of production. In short, as digital technologies are made more effective in terms of energy consumption and resource use, the more resources IT firms will have to develop new lines of application and business. As a result, these technologies get taken up at even higher rates and therefore consume higher levels of energy and resources. As Ritwick Ghosh (2021) concludes: 'the history of technologically driven efficiency gains warns us – what we gain with improved efficiency, we typically lose (and more) with increased consumption'.

Other experts openly question the scale and speed at which decarbonizing activities can be enacted. Sustainable energy experts such as Vaclav Smil (2022) are at pains to point out how these proposed sustainable energy systems are based around extraordinary (if not fantastical) increases in the levels of production that would depend on technologies and processes that are yet be invented. In short, even if the world's corporations and governments undergo an abrupt pivot toward sustainable energy, there is neither the time, resources nor technologies required for a successful transition to green energy.

Second, even if such green technical fixes are achievable, it is argued that they will have inherent side-effects and second-order environmental consequences. For example, some of the recent proposals for improving energy efficiency depend on the mining of rare earth materials such as tantalum that are in dangerously short supply. Another common complaint is how the tech industry 'fetish' for decarbonizing distracts from other unaddressed problems of material extraction, excessive water consumption and e-waste (Kneese 2023). Doubts are also raised over the feasibility of the carbon-related aspects of 'greening' tech industry activities. While many of the largest tech companies are relying heavily on offsetting emissions through strategies such as tree planting to meet their 2030 commitments, these are not viable reduction actions given the huge quantities of carbon being talked about (New Climate Institute 2022). As environmental scientist Bonnie Waring (2021) unequivocally puts it, 'there aren't enough trees in the world to offset society's carbon emissions – and there never will be'.

It is therefore important to keep reminding ourselves that the solutionist bluster of Green Tech, Clean Tech and similar is all based on questionable claims about decoupling economic growth and resource consumption from environmental pressures – what Marquis (2024) describes as the 'illusory goal of unfettered growth *and* sustainability'. Many critics see this as a classic corporate bait-and-switch – a way for tech firms to distract from broader environmental failings while also improving their market appeal and attracting investors. Mel Gregg, who founded Intel's Sustainability Taskforce, called out the corporation's claim to be 'water positive' as an attempt to 'apparently offset the dubious practice of building large manufacturing facilities in water-distressed regions' (Gregg and Strengers 2024). Gregg similarly dismisses Big Tech claims of 'net zero' as simply 'another differentiating move in the competition to acquire customers' (Gregg and Strengers 2024). All told, we need to remain highly sceptical of claims by the IT industry to be greening up its act. As Paul Schütze (2024) puts it:

> Sustainable [tech] is the technical solution to the climate crisis from a techno-solutionist vantage point simply reproducing the status quo. The enthusiasm for sustainable [tech] primarily serves hegemonic interests . . . if we want true climate action, sustainable [tech] is not the way to go.

Of course, there is nothing wrong in pushing for alternative energy sources and looking for ways of reducing carbon emissions. However, these actions alone do not excuse the continued growth of digital excess at all other costs. All told, there are good grounds to anticipate that these Green Tech efforts will prove to be of limited effectiveness, and perhaps even be counterproductive. For example, in light of concerns over ocean heating and the impact of increased carbon dioxide atmospheric concentration on marine environments, it makes little sense to fill our oceans with data centres. Similarly, there is little sense in using AI to monitor deforestation if the continued functioning of AI is implicated as a driver of deforestation. As Sasha Luccioni reasons: 'Fundamentally speaking, if you do want to save the planet with AI, you have to consider also the environmental footprint [of AI] . . . It doesn't make sense to burn a forest and then use AI to track deforestation' (cited in Stokel-Walker 2023).

Why these promises might not be enough

Of course, many people find understandable comfort in believing that the IT industry has solutions to mounting environmental issues. As Siddarth and Nabben (2021) put it, 'in an age of human-led mass extinction and climate catastrophe, the dream of a technological higher power saving us from ourselves is tempting'. Indeed, the IT industry is certainly not alone in hoping that the coming together of high-tech and green ambitions will prove transformative. Such thinking also underpins current enthusiasm for fast-tracking innovations such as carbon capture and storage technology, nuclear-fusion energy, lab-grown meat, wind farms and even solar geoengineering. A faith in Green Tech is a popular stance in environmental thinking across the political spectrum – from 'eco-modern Marxists' to 'green capitalists' (Ahern 2023a).

Yet such thinking dangerously reduces the complexities of climate crisis to a series of technical problems that can be codified and resolved. As Tega Brain and Sam Lavinge (2024) put it, 'it is convenient for the tech industry that the pursuit of "net zero" is a massive computational challenge'. Moreover, this mindset limits our conception of viable actions to straightforward matters of increasing efficiencies. This is evident in arguments that the carbon emissions problems of AI can be addressed by more efficient data centre operations, optimized AI life cycles, and more efficient hardware. All this stands in stark contrast to the less straightforward argument that the climate crisis actually requires drastically reduced energy and resource consumption throughout the Global North:

> The technocratic myth is that decarbonization must centre on the invention and deployment of new technologies ... [T]hey lull us into the belief that new tech can simply be scaled up and plugged in. It's a state of mind that reflects our own condition of alienation. (Fleckenstein and Dale 2023)

This is the dilemma at the heart of any proposals for Green Tech and Tech for Good – how can we trust the tech industry to come good and get things right after decades of *not* getting things right? Are we prepared to gamble that these new technological fixes can somehow make a substantive difference? The response from the tech classes to all the potentially catastrophic problems laid out in Chapter 1 is clear – we just need to hold our nerve and wait for a few breakthroughs that will allow us to fully benefit from the digital age with none of its initial drawbacks. In light of everything argued so far in this book, this seems too good to be true. To reiterate a point made in Chapter 1, it is time to be calling out the promises of the tech industry for what they are – self-serving moves in support of the continuation of growth-fixated digital capitalism.

Indeed, there are many good reasons not to take reassurances that 'tech will save us' at face value, not least because of the consistently poor track record amongst Big Tech corporations and other IT industry actors in realizing such ambitions. For example, in terms of the Green Tech agendas just outlined, Big Tech (like most corporations and governments) have long histories of failing to meet their long-term pledges around carbon emissions and e-waste. As Tamara Kneese (2023) notes:

> corporate net zero goals are built on speculative, and often empty, promises. Most companies are failing to meet their targets and would have to redouble their emissions reductions efforts to be carbon negative by 2030 . . . Carbon offsets are essentially scams, another example of a technologically driven solution to a social problem; a mere 4 percent of carbon offsets actually remove CO_2 from the atmosphere. In some cases, carbon offsets actively harm marginalised people and endangered species in parts of the world that are already facing catastrophic climate impacts.

Perhaps the most significant barrier to these ambitions for Green Tech and Tech for Good being successfully realized is the growth-driven motives of IT industry actors. All the goals and ambitions outlined in this chapter face a clear clash of priorities and motivations, with any IT industry actions underpinned ultimately by a concern with economic growth. Tackling societal inequalities or transitioning to renewable energy are not sufficiently lucrative enough challenges for the private sector to take fully seriously (Christophers 2024). Indeed, even the most progressive corporate entities 'must prioritise the interests of investors, shareholders, and paying customers, which may or may not align with any vision of "a better internet" for the rest of us' (Ruddock and Donovan 2023: 119). Of course, economic-led agendas do not stop tech industry actors from espousing commitments to developing 'Tech for Good' or striving toward 'better' forms of tech sustainability. Yet beneath these headline ambitions, vague notions of 'good' and 'better' will almost always fail to disclose the beneficiaries of these benefits. As such, we need to challenge such claims by asking the key question of 'better for who?' As Jenna Ruddock and Joan Donovan (2023: 118) put it, '[better] for the public? For the company's shareholders? For paying customers? For advertisers? Where do those visions overlap – and, more tellingly, where do they diverge?'

Repoliticizing conversations around digital 'good'

The extent to which we should be prepared to trust the intentions of Big Tech and other IT industry actors remains questionable. The more cynical among us might argue that the tech community knows full well that these issues of societal and environmental sustainability do not have any easy digital solutions. Every corporate promise to transform society and save the environment is offset by reports of tech billionaires investing in remote ranches in New Zealand, building bunkers in Hawaii and furiously funding attempts to kickstart commercial forays into space travel and interplanetary settlement. As Kate Soper observes:

> The imminence of ecological calamity is acknowledged by some of Silicon Valley's richest inhabitants, who are desperately seeking personalised technological escape routes from what they call the 'Event' (the rising waters, social chaos and anarchy of future environmental breakdown). (2023: 40)

Regardless of Jeff Bezos' or Mark Zuckerberg's personal commitments to seeing through their corporations' promises, it is difficult to see how current forms of tech solutionism will radically alter the status quo and/or offer a different set of options from what has got us into the present predicament. Seen in this light, hopes that 'tech will save us' are perhaps best understood as a form of what Robert Rosenberger calls 'spectatorial utopianism' – the token acceptance that the problem exists while attempting to divert attention away from the need to engage with the politics of what needs to be done. As Rosenberger puts it, 'this kind of argument should be recognized for what it is: a call against active problem solving based on contentious assumptions about the nature of technology' (2023: 1965).

The tech industry 'solutions' advanced in this chapter certainly distract from any acknowledgment that societal divisions and climate crisis are being driven by contemporary forms of capitalism with their emphasis on relentless economic growth. Instead, these solutions undeniably work in the entrenched interests of capital. Thus, the ideas of Green Tech and Tech for Good understandably appeal to Big Tech and IT industry interests but might also be argued to resonate with an environmental lobby funded by billionaire philanthropic foundations and whose default tendency is to work with – rather than against – capitalism. As Andrew Ahern (2023a) contends, 'pinning the blame on capitalism, specifically, as the cause of our ecological crisis has been a bridge too far for many environmentalists . . . mainstream environmentalism seems to believe capitalism can be "greened"'. In contrast, however, there are good grounds to argue that the continuation of digital capitalism through promises of Green Tech and Tech for Social Good is an ultimately destructive path to be pursuing. We should not be fooled into thinking that Big Tech and the broader IT industrial complex is sympathetic to planetary and environmental needs. Instead, all the 'innovations' outlined in this chapter might more accurately be seen as attempts by Big Tech corporations to continue profiting from current forms of digital technology for as long as they can. Anyone hoping for genuinely radical change is going to have to look elsewhere.

Conclusions

At the moment, the orthodox response to the mounting problems of digital sustainability outlined in Chapter 1 is to trust the tech industry to make good on its promises of 'Green Tech' and 'Tech for Social Good'. In short, we are encouraged to believe that there is nothing to be worried about, that societal and environmental problems can be solved by intensifying and accelerating current forms of digital innovation. In contrast, this chapter has laid out various reasons to think otherwise. This is not to say that we should reject every tech solution that is being put forward. There are certainly ways in which the spirit of Tech for Social Good might be taken up by marginalized and disadvantaged communities in ways that promote genuine empowerment and contextual nuance. Similarly, current discussions around Green Tech touch on areas of innovation that might well be reappropriated in less exploitative ways. For example, Chapter 6 will return to the idea of embedding digital technology within natural ecosystems, albeit not in ways that litter the seabed with data centres conveniently located next to the most profitable markets.

Indeed, it might be argued that some of these corporate projects and commitments should continue in the short term. Any transition to digital degrowth will be a relatively slow and gradual process. If Amazon and Google want to push for solar and wind energy over the next decade, then there is no reason to stop them. Similarly, if AI models have already been developed to address harmful levels of energy consumption then, again, it seems sensible to make the most of any immediate gains. Nevertheless, in the longer term we clearly need to think differently. In the long term these mainstream responses are woefully insufficient – driven by interests that are keen to promote (and profit from) the continued growth-driven digitization of society for decades to come.

So, rather than get distracted by talk of net-zero data centres and carbon neutral computing, we need to develop more substantial responses to what is clearly a damaging and unsustainable trajectory. If everything covered in this chapter is ultimately not enough, then what do we want? The next chapter considers how issues of digital unsustainability are being addressed beyond mainstream responses from IT industry and policy communities. What are groups with little or nothing to gain from the continuation of the status quo thinking of? How can we 'deepen, rather than flatten, the imaginary of what the problems and solutions are' (Jansen 2023: 57)?

3
Beginning to Think Differently About Digital Technology

Introduction

It is time to start thinking differently about digital technology. While visions of 'Green Tech' and 'Tech for Good' offer promises of quick painless solutions to the problems laid out in Chapter 1, in essence these are little more than business-as-usual proposals that effectively grant licence for digital capitalism to continue growing. Considering the rapid and relentless expansion of Big Tech since the 2000s, it seems risky (if not outright reckless) to pin our futures on grand pledges and hubristic commitments from growth-hungry corporations to suddenly start acting more responsibly. These are certainly not actors that have an interest in challenging the status quo.

Of course, the act of thinking differently is easier said than done. Even people fully committed to all sorts of other radical reform tend to have a blind spot when it comes to digital technology. Indeed, seemingly trenchant forms of tech criticism usually remain grounded in the assumption that 'it will all somehow persist' (Crary 2022: 47). Yet, history tells us that there is no reason to presume the permanency of the digital condition. The end of the digital age is no more unthinkable than the end of the Dark Ages, the Renaissance or Ice Age. In light of climate warming, global pandemics and rising geopolitical instability, it seems foolhardy to assume that anything is 'here to stay', let alone something as fragile and finite as the silicon chip.

So, how else might we set about this process of radically rethinking digital technology? This chapter considers various ways in which digital technology has been reimagined in the recent past along lines of sustainability, environmental change and social justice. These all offer hope that the current dominance of growth-driven digital excess can be challenged effectively. In other words, this chapter makes the argument that there are powerful precedents for working toward a different politics of digital technology. In particular, it introduces some ideas and ideals that can help reorient our sense of why we might want to continue to have digital technology in our lives, albeit in radically different forms. The challenge, then, is to think how different forms of digital technology might be developed in ways that are significantly more societally and environmentally sustainable in their material forms, logics and underpinning values.

Imagining new values for new technology

These notions of value and values are key starting points for any discussion around the future of digital technology. Being clear about what is wrong with contemporary forms of digital technology and being confident that change is possible is only half the battle. The more difficult question to be tackled is what we want to see instead. This is clearly something that needs to be collectively deliberated and decided upon. What broadly might we want to see digital technologies being used for in our societies, and with what guiding principles and ideals?

As implied throughout the past two chapters, the idea of radically rethinking digital technology is actually a matter of thinking about wider changes that need to be made across all aspects of society and the arrangement of everyday life. As such, the challenge that we now need to address is imagining a new mode of digital technology that explicitly fits with broader ambitions for the conditioning of human, material and political life along kinder, fairer and environmentally sensitive lines. This requires a sociotechnical framing of digital technology as outlined in Chapter 1 – from the materials used in the construction of hardware to the conditions in which technology is made accessible and used. It requires encouraging and stimulating different digitally informed (as opposed to digitally driven) practices that reinvigorate people's relationships with digital technology, and fundamentally alter how people understand digital technology in terms of its impact, intent and purpose. These are changes that not only challenge the 'what', but also the 'why' and the 'how' of digital technology.

In this sense, the opening chapters of this book have already begun to sketch out a sense of what a better mode of digital technology might look like if we reject the imperatives of digital capitalism and growth. To continue a few themes that have emerged so far, we might desire . . .

- a mode of digital technology that is not in thrall to the exhortative and extractive logics of contemporary capitalism and imperatives of growth. Instead, we might look forward to different ways of organizing the digital – based on solidarity and planning, rather than compulsive accumulation (Fleckenstein and Dale 2023).
- a mode of digital technology that exists to benefit everyone – not least those who are already marginalized and disadvantaged. This would be digital technology that is not built upon logics of individual benefit, standardization, monitoring, manipulation or control; a digital tech that is trusting, caring and kind – that empowers the neediest, advantages the most disadvantaged, and is based around the common good.
- a mode of digital technology that is in harmony with the material elements and the natural environments that it is born from. This would be digital tech that is not reliant on the depletion of natural resources, extractive capitalism, exploitative labour, wasteful consumption and toxic disposal practices; a digital tech that can be sustained within current (and future) environmental limits. This requires reimagining digital technology along material and planetary lines, bringing 'hypermodern centres of technology and power into relationship with far-flung glaciers, forests, oceans and tundra' (Davies 2022).
- a mode of digital technology that is developed and implemented to assist us in our efforts to cope with the complex challenges of social inequalities and climate change. These would not be speculative technology-centric 'solutions' that distract from other attempts to address these issues. Instead,

Beginning to Think Differently About Digital Technology   43

they would be technologies that are part of wider efforts to address the social and environmental challenges of our times.

There is a lot to unpack in these dot points. To reiterate one of the main conclusions reached in Chapter 1, this is a call to reimagine the value of digital technology in terms of social and environmental good rather than capitalist notions of profit, return on investment, stock prices and establishing ever more lucrative markets. At the same time, this is a call to reconstitute digital technologies on a new ethical basis of values – ideals and ambitions that support acts of collective well-being, mutual solidarity, care for what we already have, and a shared obligation to other living things and the planet.

First, then, is the need to engage with technological change as a shared, communal process rather than an individual obligation. This requires the rejection of prevailing Silicon Valley/Western framings of digital technology as a matter of individual consumption, and instead reframing digital technology as a collectively determined endeavour. Above all, this implies the sustained and genuine involvement of marginalized, vulnerable groups in determining the focus and form of new technology-related interventions. In other words, if tech *is* going to be leveraged for social good, this is something that everyone needs to be involved in. Approaching the societal implementation of digital technology as a collective, shared endeavour opens up possibilities of radically rethinking digital technology in terms of a social movement with collective benefits and shared jeopardy. Of course, it is common to argue that digital technologies should be focused on the needs and demands of communities. Yet 'communities' can often be exclusionary and conservative, lacking in reciprocity, solidarity and trust. Developing genuinely empowering and emancipatory forms of digital technology therefore needs to be engaged in as a form of radical collective technopolitics.

Second, we need to acknowledge that rethinking and reframing digital technology is something that should be initiated within local contexts rather than led by transnational corporations, national governments and/or state actors with little vested interest in initiating sustainable, fair and enriching forms of change. This suggests adopting approaches from post-development thinking that propose actions that are 'not rooted in centralized, industrial growth, but localized development leveraging local resources and knowledge' (Sharma, Kumar and Nardi 2023: 1). Here, for example, we might like to follow Erik Olin Wright's (2010) suggestion that these local actions can be seen as: (i) interstitial (i.e. building alternatives in the cracks of existing systems); (ii) symbiotic (i.e. working within systems to reform them); and (iii) ruptural (i.e. disrupting and fighting against dominant systems).

Third, we need to embrace the idea of refining digital technology use as a progressive and innovative act. Indeed, reassessing our relationships with digital technology along refined, restrained lines needs to be seen as a defiantly forward-looking move, rather than a meekly regressive concession. This requires developing critical consciousness of how our societies are currently set up to facilitate and normalize the over-consumption of digital technology, as well as the ways in which technological products and services are designed to engender endless engagement and use. Seen in these terms, the act of scaling back societal dependencies on digital technology is something that we can actively desire, rather than something we are forced into.

Fourth, we need to ensure that the various costs and benefits of how we choose to reimagine digital technology along more 'sustainable' lines are apportioned fairly, and do not excessively disadvantage the already disadvantaged. This suggests rethinking digital tech in terms of distributive justice – fostering sustainable and socially appropriate forms of digital technology for disadvantaged groups who stand to benefit most from the continued use of digital technology (and, conversely, stand to lose most from the enforced absence of digital technology). All told, refashioning forms of digital technology that are more societally and environmentally sustainable does not simply equate with making less harmful uses of digital technology. Instead, it pushes us to think about how to make less harmful uses of technology for more just outcomes.

Fifth, there is the need for a decolonial sensibility when reimagining what digital technology might be. While the pursuit of these aims needs to be a worldwide undertaking, we need to be careful to distinguish between different parts of the world. Indeed, many of the social harms and most of the environmental burdens referred to over the past two chapters fall disproportionately on the poorest parts of the world and the most disadvantaged populations. Ultimately, establishing an alternative technological regime requires people around the world to work together toward the establishment of reparative modes of digital technology that are rooted in the interests and experiences of what are increasingly described in climate discussions as the 'most affected people and areas'. These are the populations and places that are disproportionately affected by the climate crisis, and that have been historically disadvantaged by the development of digital capitalism. This includes people living in poverty and Indigenous Peoples, as well as parts of the Global South without basic digital infrastructure but whose lands and peoples have borne the brunt of resource extraction, e-waste and the imposition of data centres. Above all, this requires a clean break from hegemonic Silicon Valley thinking rooted in Euro-centric views of innovation and technology.

What can degrowth add to rethinking the digital?

This brings us to the main focus of this book – bringing degrowth thinking to bear on the question of how to rethink digital technology along lines that are socially and environmentally oriented. First, then, it is worth tracking back a little and developing a sense of the broad tenets of degrowth thinking. While the term has come to prominence since the 2000s, degrowth thinking has roots in writing during the early 1970s around 'limits to growth' (Meadows et al. 1972; see also Schumacher 1973), which first popularized the idea that exponential economic growth might well prove to be unsustainable given the planet's finite resources. Other contemporary thinkers such as André Gorz also advanced arguments that achieving a better balance with the earth would require a 'no-growth' or 'degrowth' (décroissance) of material production (Lenzen 2024). At the same time, various writers initiated the idea of ecological economics, stressing what Herman Daly (1972) termed the 'case against continuous exponential growth'. Earlier still, Kenneth Boulding (1966) had warned of the need for economic thinking to move away from 'cowboy' visions of limitless frontiers and instead embrace a 'spaceman' vision of the planet based around efficient management of limited resources. Tellingly, Boulding wrote sixty years ago of the need to develop different forms of technology which were non-toxic and not reliant on exhaustible materials.

46   Digital Degrowth

Following on from these beginnings, the term 'décroissance' was revitalized through the writing of Serge Latouche and others during the 2000s. Since then, a loose and diffuse range of academics, ecological economists, environmentalists and activists have picked up these ideas. Now degrowth thinking is being championed by a wide range of groups and collectives, with writers such as Jason Hickel, Giorgos Kallis, Tim Jackson, François Schneider, Federico Demaria and Kōhei Saitō working hard over the past decade to develop and popularize the concept. The degrowth movement now encompasses those who identify themselves as working in the area of ecological economics through to various forms of utopian socialism and anarchism. As we shall see across the remainder of this book, degrowth continues to be a broad church that is interpreted widely.

That said, the basic premise of degrowth is straightforward enough. As Kallis et al. summarize:

> Degrowth makes the case that we have to produce and consume differently, and also less. That we have to share more and distribute more fairly, while the pie shrinks. To do so in ways that support pleasurable and meaningful lives in resilient societies and environments requires values and institutions that produce different kinds of persons and relations. (2020: 5)

As with most simple sounding summaries, there is a lot packed into this short definition. While degrowthers are concerned with descaling harmful modes of production and consumption, this is not simply a call to do less of what we are already doing. Instead, degrowth is a call to start doing different things. More specifically, degrowth is a call to find different ways of doing things that lead to more meaningful, relational and equitable outcomes. Despite its reductive-sounding prefix, degrowth is focused firmly on working out ways toward positive change and rebalancing the use of resources.

Key here are ideas of progressing in 'low impact' ways and embracing principles of 'voluntary simplicity'. At an individual level, this can be seen as 'reducing one's environmental impact in an emancipatory and intentional way whenever, and however, possible' (Liegey and Nelson 2020: 58). Yet, degrowth thinking acknowledges that any changes in individual behaviour need to be set against collective well-being and ensuring the equitable rebalancing of societal systems in ways that do not further disadvantage the already disadvantaged. The challenge that degrowth therefore poses is straightforward: 'how we can enable societies to prosper without growth, to ensure a just and ecological future?' (Hickel et al. 2022: 403).

Here, it is worth considering these basic principles in a little more detail. First, as its name suggests, a core principle of degrowth is its rejection of ongoing economic growth as the dominant basis for societal progress and/or human welfare. Degrowth starts from the premise that we currently live in a world predicated upon perpetual growth – 'the idea that firms, industries and nations must increase production every year, regardless of whether it is needed' (Hickel et al. 2022: 400). As Chapters 1 and 2 have already argued in terms of the tech sector, the problem with this endless quest for growth is that it results in energy, materials and resources being consumed at unsustainable rates. It also results in the pursuit of innovation primarily to chase further investment and profit, rather than to address any genuine societal needs. Degrowth thinkers therefore challenge us to break from this cycle of ever-increasing production of goods and services, and instead force an 'equitable downscaling' of economic production and consumption (Sekulova et al. 2013).

This is not a blanket argument against all types of growth, rather that societies should not pursue unnecessary growth that is motivated by desires to maximize profits and wealth. Degrowthers support the increase of production where it can achieve social and ecological benefits. Degrowth is simply a call to break the cycle of unnecessary growth – the pursuit of growth for the sake of profit, and economic obsessions with national gross domestic products rather than actual social conditions. In this sense, degrowthers contend that limiting ourselves only to necessary and beneficial growth is likely to lead to massive contractions and downscaling of unnecessary economic and industrial activity, as well as substantial reductions in the materials and resources needed to support societies. Degrowth therefore pushes for forms of voluntary simplicity – ways of life based around 'consciously minimising wasteful and resource-intensive consumption' (Alexander 2015: 133) to levels that are most appropriate and beneficial for all.

Second, it is important not to presume that degrowth is simply an appeal to use less of what we already have, or a call for the collective takeover of existing resources and techniques. Instead, degrowth calls for the reassessment of how communities choose to appropriate resources in ways that are sensitive to their local contexts and circumstances – 'purposively slow[ing] things down in order to minimize harm to humans and earth systems' (Kallis et al. 2020: viii). An allied degrowth principle arises from Heidegger's idea of releasement (*gelassenheit*), broadly understood as a willingness to let things be as they are and resist the compulsion to improve everything (Heikkurinen 2018). This notion of slowing down, doing less and not striving to constantly improve things is one element of degrowth that can feel particularly unsettling for many people, especially in Western cultures of ever-accelerating progress. Nevertheless, degrowthers are adamant that a slower pace of life is key to 'producing less negative socioecological impacts than existing market systems' (Kallis et al. 2020: 62).

In particular, working along slower and more bounded lines is understood to bolster people's capacity to work in ways that involve cooperation, coproduction, collective deliberation and local self-determination. Such principles take time to genuinely establish but are crucial to degrowth ambitions of living as modestly as possible in ways that are equitable and life-affirming. Degrowth therefore pushes for making time to attend to the needs of all people (and all things) within a local community. In this sense, many practical applications of degrowth philosophies involve practices such as bartering, exchange, time-banking and skill-swapping, alongside collaborative forms of consumption, maintenance, repair and sharing.

Finally, as these latter examples suggest, degrowth promotes a defiantly post-capitalist agenda – seeking to develop alternatives to market forces and profit as the primary organizing principles of social life. This has been a key element of degrowth thinking since the beginning, especially in terms of the incompatibility of environmental goals and what Mike Kidron (1966) bemoaned sixty years ago as the 'growth fetishism' of modern capitalism. Degrowthers therefore contend that thinking and acting beyond capitalism is an essential step in addressing the social, environmental and ecological crisis that the world currently faces. Capitalism offers no imperative to meaningfully tackle issues of social disadvantage and suffering. Indeed, capitalism is built inherently around the idea of there being winners and losers, those who prosper and those who do not. Similarly, capitalism offers no imperative to stop extracting resources and exploiting the planet for profit. As Andrew Ahern (2023a) reasons: 'What is unique about capitalism . . . is the *rift* it creates between human and natural systems. In short, capitalism develops and maintains its productive technologies by also draining life on earth: human and otherwise.'

Taking a degrowth perspective

In bringing these ideas into correspondence with the usually hype-heavy world of digital technology, it is important not to misread 'degrowth' as implying a retrogressive 'return to a primitive past' (Liegey and Nelson 2020: 49). Degrowth is not an argument for a form of 'forced deprivation' or 'martyred self-denial or constraining human potential' (Kallis et al. 2020: 18, 109). Instead, degrowth strives for the progressive reorientation of everyday life in ways that are empowering, sustainable and pleasurable for far greater numbers of people and communities than is possible under market conditions. As such, degrowth is focused on adopting new practices, relations and institutions that work toward progressive social change and values of ecological integrity and social justice. As Liegey and Nelson (2020: 36) contend, 'degrowth invites you to rethink your values and relations with respect to socio-cultural impacts . . . in short to re-evaluate your use of everything'.

Degrowth thinking obviously is applicable to all areas of modern life. Yet, at this point it is important to stress that degrowth does not offer a straightforward blueprint or manifesto for change. There is no ten-point plan or prescribed degrowth doctrine to follow. Instead, degrowth is a provocation to radically rethink how communities choose to do things, as well as the resources that are drawn upon to do these things. This raises a range of questions that need to be carefully worked through. For example, what areas of production might be deemed less necessary, or overly destructive, and therefore in need of scaling down? Is there justification in a degrowth society for mass-produced meat, fast fashion, weapons manufacturing, privately owned cars or aviation? Which areas of socially and environmentally beneficial production – such as renewable energy and universal healthcare – might be expanded? What other forms of slowing down and scaling back – such as a universal basic income or a three-day working week – might improve people's overall quality of life and well-being?

Degrowthers accept that none of these transitions is likely to be smooth, and that some of them might not work out as expected. Yet, this uncertainty should not deter us from trying to do things differently. In this sense, degrowth is an invitation for ongoing dialogue and a trial-and-error approach, rather than a clearly defined agenda for immediate change and upheaval. Indeed, it is accepted that any practical degrowth transition will involve diversifying how things are done, introducing localized, cooperative modes of production, consumption and caring that might complement and eventually challenge the existing forms of large-scale production that currently dominate. Crucially, this will require numerous small-scale local experiments, with local communities working to disentangle themselves from clearly unsustainable but established ways of doing things.

These ideas of scaling back and self-determination mean that degrowth is very much about encouraging change at a local level. Degrowth pushes for communities to work together to explore and refine grassroots practices that are appropriate to their local contexts and circumstances. Degrowth encourages people to share ideas with those around them and pay attention to where these small ideas begin to work together in synergy, and how wider connections might arise between many different local read-justments. Crucially, then, the impetus for these changes needs to be led by bottom-up public mobilization. This will initially require individuals, groups and communities to self-organize into grassroots networks, building alliances amongst those who have no real self-interest in the continuation of contemporary capital-ism as it currently stands. Large corporations and governments have little incentive to lead efforts to change the status quo. Any lasting change is therefore most likely to be initiated outside these large institutions, which will need to be subsequently forced to fall into line through sheer weight of public demand for change.

Some core degrowth principles to take forward

So, how can we start setting about reimagining what digital tech-nology might look like within these altered conditions? While approaches to degrowth vary, a few core ideas have obvious affinity with rethinking what digital degrowth might look like. First is the idea of the commons, and the associated principle of 'commoning'. In brief, this involves the management of shared resources that are open to all members of a community. The process of commoning is familiar from the shared access to and governance of natural resources such as parklands, forests, rivers, fisheries and other open spaces, as well as shared musical repertoires, folklore and other cultural knowledges. These are all instances where people come together to create, manage and share resources, with all members of a community collaboratively working out norms and rules of use, and other ways that these shared resources might be best governed and regulated.

Seeing technology as a commons therefore directly challenges the sense of digital resignation that there is nothing that people can do to change digital technology. In contrast, technology as commons is something that all people can have a part in collectively deciding. As Helfrich and Bollier put it: 'a resource *becomes* a commons when it is taken care of by a community or network. The community, resource, and rules are all an integrated whole' (2015: 75). In this sense, the commons is not a 'free-for-all', but an arrangement of mutually agreed upon rules, boundaries, sanctions and social norms – what is sometimes referred to as shared stewardship. Key here are practices of regular communication, negotiation and experimenting. Commoning offers means of mutual benefit and co-governance 'which are significantly more equal, transparent, democratic and sustainable than those driven by the logic of the market' (Liegey and Nelson 2020: ix).

A second core component of degrowth that chimes with rethinking digital technology is the idea of conviviality, drawing heavily on the work of Ivan Illich. This proposes a radically different relationship between people and the 'tools' they encounter. Crucially, Illich's notion of 'tool' encompasses everything from basic objects and artefacts through to more complex machines and technical resources, institutions and infrastructures (from a screwdriver through to a nationwide transportation system). Illich contended that under industrial capitalism these tools work in ways that are usually exploitative and disempowering, reducing people to the status of operator, user or consumer, and deliberately impairing their freedom of thought and creative action. These tools are usually closed off to non-experts – either made unnecessarily complicated or physically inaccessible – meaning

52   Digital Degrowth

that most people must rely on a body of specialists to reconfigure or repair the tools. Illich (1973) referred to these as 'manipulative tools'.

In contrast, 'convivial tools' are those that are 'understandable, manageable and controllable by their users' (Kallis, Demaria and D'Alisa 2015: 8). These are tools that can be used in self-determined ways, that are not prefigured and controlled by others, and not reliant on small bodies of specialists with proprietary technical expertise and resources. Crucially, these are tools that exist (as much as is possible) outside of corporate and government control, and instead are resources that people can use together – sharing skills, expertise and experience, and collaboratively working out ways these tools might be used. This is sometimes described as a case of 'Do It Ourselves' (an improvement on the more individualistic notion of 'Do It Yourself'). Illich acknowledged a need for industrial production but pushed for balancing this against people's own creative capacities to do more together. Indeed, Andrea Vetter (2018) describes convivial tools as imbuing values of 'relatedness' in that they 'bring about things between people' such as trust, community and respect. In this sense, convivial tools are open to reconfiguration and 'tinkering', with people given a leading role in shaping the life cycles of the tools they use.

A third associated feature is 'autonomy'. Much of the previous description of convivial tools relates to the idea of autonomous values and practices – where people can satisfy their own needs, rather than fitting around arbitrary 'needs' imposed by others. As Kōhei Saitō puts it, degrowth thinking seeks to 'foster the development of technologies that enable people to manage their lives themselves' (2024: 147). Illich referred to this as 'vernacular subsistence', involving, for example, tools that can operate outside of external infrastructures (such as a centralized energy system), or that can be easily maintained and repaired. Crucially, this is not an individualistic notion of autonomy, but an ethical valuing of individual autonomy that arises from personal interdependence with others. In this sense, degrowth imagines groups of autonomous people working together to satisfy their own needs, while also providing each other with mutual support, assistance and solidarity.

This leads on to a final set of underpinning principles that relate to matters of care and caring. The notion of care takes a

Beginning to Think Differently About Digital Technology   53

few different forms in degrowth thinking, not least in the idea of groups of people taking care *of* resources. It is this sense that 'a resource becomes a commons when it is taken care of by a community or network' (Helfrich and Bollier 2015: 75). At the same time there is the idea of providing care *for* others – working to sustain a spirit of community welfare and solidarity, and lessening the vulnerability of others. In this sense, any degrowth action is undertaken in order to increase collective sustenance and well-being – in contrast to the deeply divisive sense of individualized entitlement and individualized benefit that is fostered by capitalism. All told, degrowth thinking foregrounds ideas of mutual concern for others, mutual respect and a general emphasis on the enrichment of human relations.

Moving beyond criticisms of degrowth

All these principles of commoning, conviviality, autonomy and care have obvious relevance to rethinking digital technology. In Chapter 4 we will apply these ideals to digital technology and outline what 'digital degrowth' might mean. Chapters 5 and 6 will then work through a wide range of ideas for what this digital degrowth might look like in practice. However, until recently, there has been a notable reluctance to put degrowth thinking together with ambitions for digital reform, especially amongst degrowth communities and in the wider field of environmental economics. Curiously, digital technology continues to be something that is not much talked about in discussions of degrowth. This book is an attempt to change this, but before we dive headlong into thinking what degrowth might mean for digital technology (and vice versa), it is worth concluding this chapter by reflecting a little on why so many people seem to think that degrowth is a decidedly bad idea.

One common criticism is that degrowth is an implicit call for imposed austerity – a denial of the most significant advances that humans have made over the past hundred years and an enforced return to some sort of 'back to the land' primitivism. One vocal advocate of this position is the geographer Matt Huber (2023), who dismisses degrowth as a form of stealth 'ecological austerity' which unnecessarily looks to constrain 'human potential' (notably of the working classes). Other critics characterize this as 'forced degrowth' which can only be achieved through 'an authoritarian regime of global planning' (Driscoll 2024). Elsewhere are criticisms that degrowth is little more than intellectual posturing amongst a narrow clique of European middle-class academics with little relevance to the rest of the world. It is also argued by some left-leaning critical commentators that degrowth is simply a fantastical position – an unrealistic abdication of engaging in more immediate, messy struggles over class welfare, the rise of populist nationalism, neo-fascism and other current sociopolitical crises. As David Griscom (2022) contends: 'degrowth isn't realism, it's a pessimistic belief that we can't build a post-capitalist society without global sacrifice and suffering'. Alongside these misgivings, other critics are simply triggered into feeling that degrowth is too bleak, too extreme or simply overly negative.

Many of these accusations are easily rebuffed, or else are issues that degrowthers are aware of and working to redress. In fairness, degrowth thinking is primarily European, middle class and academic in its origins, and clearly needs to be subsumed and adapted by more diverse publics around the world. In this regard, we are already seeing worldwide networks of local degrowth movements being established to push degrowth into a new internationalist phase of action. Otherwise, most of these knee-jerk criticisms hold little water. As has been discussed throughout this chapter, degrowth aims to ensure that the majority of the world's population is better off materially and spiritually than at present, as well as ensuring the protection of our planet and environment. Any deprivation or austerity is only likely to be felt by the wealthiest middle and upper classes, who in relative terms can well afford to give up their luxuries for the greater good. Similarly, degrowth is certainly an attempt to take seriously the current era of climate change and environmental destruction. What might seem to be 'extreme' proposals simply reflect that these are not issues that can be addressed by moderate adjustments around the edges of our societies. Finally, degrowth is not something that can be forced on people – it is something that is agreed on a collective, democratic basis rather than imposed as a set blueprint or plan to be followed.

In short, degrowth is certainly a provocative notion, but it seems mostly to provoke those whose privileges it challenges. As Andrew Ahern (2023b) observes, 'degrowth pisses off all of the right people'. Tellingly, in terms of the focus of this particular book, the tech community has proven especially hostile to ideas of degrowth. As one headline in *Wired* put it: 'Why degrowth is the worst idea on the planet' (McAfee 2020). This piece extolled the greening impact of digital technologies, contrasting this with the threat of an endless 'degrowth recession' characterized by 'job losses, business closures, mortgage defaults, and other hardships and uncertainties . . . corporate and government revenue would decrease permanently, and therefore so would innovation and R&D'. Indignation at being somehow prevented from 'innovating' runs deep within the tech community. Yet, as shall be discussed in subsequent chapters, digital degrowth arguably requires greater levels of technological innovation and 'blue skies' thinking than is currently the case under digital capitalism.

However baseless their concerns, the tech classes have certainly taken a strong dislike to degrowth. Typifying such hostility is Marc Andreessen, the prominent Silicon Valley entrepreneur and investor who in 2023 released a wide-ranging 'Techno-Optimist Manifesto' that declared degrowth (alongside other 'bad ideas' such as sustainability, trust, safety and ethics) as an 'enemy' to progress. As this list implies, degrowth is seen by some factions of the tech community as a 'woke' impediment to their ambitions and aspirations. Andreessen's manifesto continues: 'our enemy is deceleration, de-growth, depopulation – the nihilistic wish, so trendy among our elites, for fewer people, less energy, and more suffering and death'. Andreessen's rant was perhaps unusual in its willingness to stridently voice such prejudices, but it is hardly atypical. Indeed, the common reaction within tech circles to mention of degrowth tends to be extreme. As Andreessen hints, one common reading of degrowth in tech circles is as a kind of 'death cult' calling for forced population decrease. While such responses are clearly unfounded, they have led to a breakdown where degrowth ideas and thinking are instinctively dismissed by many in mainstream tech circles.

Conclusions

To reiterate, degrowth is not a call for a regressive retreat to the Middle Ages or a state of digital deprivation. Instead, as Kostakis and Tsiouris put it, degrowth thinking offers a ready way to address the tension that 'high-tech is not unsustainable in its essence, but its scale and mode of production in the capitalist realm are' (2024: 1). With its emphasis on slowing down, scaling back and the collective good, degrowth can be seen as potentially powerful addition to ongoing conversations elsewhere around reimagining digital technology along more humane, fairer and caring lines – not least by those working in the areas of feminist tech, Black tech, Indigenous tech, crip technoscience and others (e.g. Toupin 2024; McIllwain 2019; Brock 2020; Kroeker 2022; Munn 2024; Shew 2023). As with these other critical tech approaches, 'in reality the degrowth movement is very future orientated – attempting to map ways out of hyper-consumption, inequality, weak democracy and the environmental crises caused by growth-driven capitalism' (Liegey and Nelson 2020: 49).

As the next chapter will go on to discuss, degrowth does not equate with a rejection of digital technology; instead it pushes us into reimagining what digital technology is, and what it might look like. In this sense, degrowth should be seen as a far more innovative position to be taking than simply plugging away at business-as-usual forms of Green Growth digital progress. If digital innovation is all about 'blue skies' and 'thinking outside of the box', then contemplating what digital degrowth might look like is as challenging and boundary-pushing as anything the IT industry is currently pushing for. After all, what could be more innovative than imagining the complete renewal and reinvention of the digital?

4
The Case for Digital Degrowth

Introduction

So, how might degrowth ideas and principles be applied to digital technology? This question is not as straightforward as it might appear. As just discussed in Chapter 3, digital technologies have so far tended to be sidelined within degrowth discussions – what Schmelzer, Vetter and Vansintjan identify as a 'void in the degrowth debate' (2022: 293). Indeed, there is still no clear degrowth consensus on technology in general; as Kerschner et al. conclude, 'the role of technology on the path towards a degrowth society is far from clear' (2018: 1619).

While some advocates enthusiastically promote the notion of 'degrowth technology' acting as an agent of transition away from growth, other degrowthers consider large technostructures to be linked inexorably with economic growth, social inequality and ecological breakdown. Indeed, Pete Howson bemoans a persistence within the degrowth literature of 'puritan-primitivist cliques that are either agnostic or hostile towards innovation', alongside many other degrowthers who appear to consider technology as 'something to be tolerated rather than actively embraced or pursued' (Howson, Crandall and Balaguer Rasillo 2021: 1). Discussions around degrowth are therefore often infused with a deeply conflicted 'love-hate relationship' with the notion of technology (Kerschner et al. 2018: 1620). While the coming together

58 Digital Degrowth

of digital technology and degrowth thinking is certainly possible, many people within the degrowth community still do not see it as an obvious fit.

The beginnings of a turn toward digital degrowth

Although many degrowthers remain undecided about the place of digital technology in their plans for a better future, tech critics and others thinking about the politics of technological change are beginning to engage with the idea of degrowth. Indeed, the past few years have seen various mentions of degrowth in discussions led by tech critics and those looking to challenge digital capitalism. For example, Christoph Becker (2023) talks of 'computing after growth', 'degrowth informatics' and the trend of 'post-growth computing'. In 2022, Brian Sutherland laid out a series of practical suggestions toward what he termed 'degrowth computing', with Vasilis Kostakis (2024) also offering practical examples in his essay 'What Technology for Degrowth?' Michael Kwet (2024) has picked up on degrowth principles as justification for establishing a 'people's tech' that moves away from the imperialist and ecocidal characteristics of the current 'Big Tech military machine'. Elsewhere we are beginning to hear talk of 'digital degrowth innovation' (Howson, Crandall and Balaguer Rasillo 2021), and Dan McQuillan (2025) has advanced the idea of 'decomputing' as 'a form of prefigurative technopolitics', pitching a vision of computing that is clearly aligned with degrowth sensibilities:

> Decomputing is a departure from AI's commitments to extractivism and scale. It invokes care for the environment through a commitment to low-power infrastructure, salvage and repair, and to deconfliction by replacing modes of computation that sediment the status quo with those drawing on principles of relationality, inclusion and respect for life.

All told, after years of degrowth discussions appearing at a tangent to the topic of digital technology, digital degrowth now seems increasingly like a good idea waiting to happen. Of course, these initial forays require a lot of elaboration and refinement, as well as a teasing out of the different strands of degrowth and ecological economics they are drawing on. For example, there is definitely a need to be clearer on the radical political intent of some of these ideas. Brian Sutherland offers some interesting practical ideas and 'proofs of concept' for how scaled-back computing can be technically enacted, but is perhaps lacking on the political intent that lies behind such designs. At the same time, there is also a need to develop tangible proposals for practical forms that digital degrowth actions might take, as well as a clearer sense of the kinds of grassroots organization that might get us there.

This chapter therefore takes a deeper dive into degrowth thinking around technology in general. Given the hyper-consumerist nature of current digital technologies and the clear harms that are associated with them, it is perhaps understandable that many degrowthers want to do away with IT altogether and start from scratch. However, as this nascent enthusiasm from outside the degrowth community suggests, there are good grounds for rethinking, rather than completely rejecting, how degrowth thinking might be put into correspondence with digital technology. As we will see, degrowth thinking abounds with ideas about how particular technologies might be developed, adopted and adapted in ways that lead to expanded freedom, creativity, autonomy and happiness. Moreover, various other efforts can be found around the margins of computer science and digital technology that are clearly 'degrowth' in spirit, if not in actual name. All told, there are good grounds to believe that bringing degrowth thinking together with the digital is possible, and indeed wholly appropriate.

Tools for conviviality

First, it is worth looking back at the many forms of pre-digital technology that fit degrowth principles. In his book *Tools for Conviviality*, Ivan Illich offered various examples such as the alphabet, printing press, typewriter and tape recorder. Writing at the beginning of the 1970s, these were all good examples of technologies that are understandable, manageable and controllable by those who use them, and that also support social engagement and creativity. As Illich noted: 'almost anybody can learn to use them, and for his own purpose. They use cheap materials. People can take them or leave them as they wish. They are not easily controlled by third parties' (1973: 64).

60 Digital Degrowth

These principles also extend to long-standing communal forms of access to tools and technologies that offer alternatives to the market, such as barter communities, local exchange trading systems and urban gardens. For example, degrowth principles are evident in the idea of local 'tool libraries' where people can borrow tools, learn and/or teach others how to use them, and contribute to their uptake. Degrowth principles are also evident in the idea of local 'repair cafés', where people can get together to work on repairing each other's objects and devices, from household appliances to clothing. Such approaches allow people to live with tools and technologies in ways that promote principles of self-sufficiency, sharing, reuse and repair.

One technology that many people see as symbolizing degrowth principles is the bicycle – a tool that is accessible to large numbers of people, offers freedom of movement, is made from durable materials, and can be easily adapted, shared and reused (Kerschner et al. 2018). Although most bicycles are industrially mass produced, they are technologies that can be maintained and repaired by laypeople without the help of external experts. Indeed, as Karin Bradley (2018: 1682) points out, bicycles can be relatively easy to understand, repair and tinker with. They are also easy to customise and modify to fit people's different needs – for example, child seats, panniers, baskets and cargo boxes can be added with minimal fuss. In these ways, a cyclist does not have to be dependent on specialists or professionals to use their bicycle. The conviviality of the bicycle has also been bolstered by people setting up community bike workshops, DIY bicycle repair studios and 'bike kitchens'. These are places – usually run along voluntary and non-profit lines – where community members can borrow tools to repair their own bikes, or perhaps build new bikes from spare parts and help others.

Of course, bicycles are not perfect – cycling remains inaccessible to people with various dis/abilities, and modern-day bike manufacturing and retailing is certainly guilty of various forms of profiteering, exploitation and environmentally unsound practices. Nevertheless, in its basic form the bicycle can be a technology that is relatively affordable and durable, as well as developed, produced and maintained through local supply chains and locally available materials (or, at least, materials that do not have to imported globally). Moreover, once manufactured, bicycles are technologies that do not substantially harm their ecological surroundings, and that can be shared and collaboratively cared for. Crucially, a society based around bicycles rather than cars would open various possibilities for different ways of living and reduced dependence on capitalist modes of production and consumption.

This is not to say that the mass uptake of cycling would lead to a fundamentally better society in and of itself. What is significant about the bicycle is its politics – the values that are implicit in cycling-informed practices, and the societal arrangements that mass use of bicycles can correspond with. The bicycle fits very well with (and can play a part in reinforcing) degrowth principles of slowing down and scaling back human practices in ways that minimize environmental impact and support living within planetary limitations. Bicycles are 'relatively non-violent' (Schumacher 1980) in the sense that they significantly reduce negative social and ecological effects in comparison to 'gigantic' technology alternatives such as mass car transportation or air travel. In terms of necessary infrastructure, bike paths are less costly and capital-intensive compared to roads. Moreover, arranging collective lifestyles around the bicycle opens the possibility of completely reorganizing our social, cultural and economic systems around 'velomobilities' rather than car-dependent automobilities (Cox 2023). To borrow a phrase from Chapter 1, the bicycle is a technology that opens up a different 'how' and 'why' of mass transportation in comparison to the currently dominant technology of the car.

Degrowth perspectives on technology

Of course, the technologies of the 2020s are not wholly comparable to bicycles, tape recorders and typewriters. Current degrowth discussions around technology now relate to everything from heat pumps to train networks. Here, then, we are seeing growing deliberation around how these technologies might have a place (or not) in any transition to degrowth living. One such overview on the relationship between degrowth and technology is provided by Jason Hickel (2023), a leading voice in the recent popularization of degrowth thinking. Hickel raises several important arguments to take forward into our own arguments around digital degrowth.

62   Digital Degrowth

First is the point that despite the negative implications of the term, degrowth is not a 'de-technology' argument. Degrowth does not imply the drastic reduction (or complete eradication) of all forms of technology use via some sort of 'back to nature' agenda. Instead, Hickel urges degrowthers to explore the roles that technology can play in addressing ecological and societal crises. However, in contrast to the ideas of Green Tech outlined in Chapter 2, these need to be new technological developments that do not perpetuate the social and ecological harms already associated with existing technology innovation. Moreover, they need to be technology developments that go together with the wider decoupling of society from capitalist growth. In this sense, technology can be an important element – but not a driving force – of future transitions to degrowth:

> In fact, degrowth scholarship *embraces* technological change and efficiency improvements, to the extent (crucially) that these are empirically feasible, ecologically coherent, and socially just. But it also recognizes that this alone will not be enough: economic and social transformations are also necessary, including a transition out of capitalism. (Hickel 2023)

The idea of pushing for forms of technology development and production that are not driven by capitalism and the imperatives of capitalist growth marks a key shift in thinking. On the one hand, this implies the reduction of all technologies that are clearly destructive and/or 'less necessary' to the well-being of people and the planet. This raises the need for cutting back on all forms of production that are clearly environmentally harmful, such as private jets, industrial beef, commercial air travel, SUVs, military weapons, cruise ships and so on. It also pushes for cutting back on all forms of production that exist primarily to support capital accumulation and elite consumption – such as advertising or fast fashion – and dramatically reducing the purchasing power of the rich.

On the other hand, this shift in thinking also pushes for refocusing our efforts toward those forms of technology that can support a transition out of capitalism. This most immediately involves prioritizing technologies that support the principle of 'well-being for all' as opposed to the mindless accumulation of capital. Examples here include the development of technologies that can support degrowth goals such as wealth redistribution,

The Case for Digital Degrowth 63

reductions in working time and the scaling back of less necessary forms of production. This also includes technologies that can be deployed in support of the establishment of universal public services and the mass redeployment of people toward state-sponsored environmental work.

At the same time, degrowth also pushes for developing technologies that might address the ecological crisis without leading to increases in aggregate growth. In this context, degrowth is certainly supportive of innovation such as solar panels, insulation, recycling and so on. Yet, unlike current 'green growth' proposals around technology, any of these desirable advances in technological efficiency must be also focused on improving levels of sufficiency and equity. Here, Hickel offers the example of how the transition to electric vehicles might be a feasible degrowth action if accompanied by efforts to scale back the private ownership of cars, to improve and expand forms of public transport, and to move societies in general away from current destructive forms of 'car culture'.

Finally, in encouraging different and expanded forms of technological progress, Hickel reiterates the point that degrowth might well prove to be more technologically expansive and innovative than current forms of capitalist technology production. Indeed, he points out that the pursuit of profit and capitalist growth imperatives actually restricts (rather than encourages) genuine technological progress and innovation. For example, it is simply not profitable to pursue various forms of technology innovation that might support developments in public transport, medicine for poor regions, or repairable devices. Instead, Hickel argues that increased public investment and democratic oversight would ensure that technology innovation is organized explicitly around social and ecological objectives. This could stimulate, for example, the development of technologies that meet the needs of currently underserved populations and that genuinely work in the interests of the public good. It could also encourage the innovative revitalization of older techniques and tools for the twenty-first century. All told, degrowth development of technology opens opportunities for the blue skies ambitions that the IT industry currently espouses, yet usually fails to fulfil.

Early degrowth perspectives on computing

So, how might we extend these ideas into the specific domain of digital technologies? Whereas the bicycle is a prominent example of a popular tool that embodies degrowth principles, this is less immediately apparent in the case of a smartphone or laptop computer. Most existing digital devices and systems are clearly 'manipulative technologies' which from a degrowth perspective need to be subject to limits. Unlike bicycle parts, it is not possible for most communities to locally manufacture silicon chips, train AI models or engage in the large-scale production processes that underpin the maintenance of current forms of digital technology. Yet, this is not to say that we should dismiss the idea of exploring the 'latent technological possibilities' of digital technologies as part of wider degrowth transitions (March 2018: 1695). Indeed, there is much that can be learnt from times and contexts where computing has not been driven by Big Tech interests and digital capitalist agendas. In this regard, we can first turn to various precedents that can be found in degrowth-adjacent thinking and writing around computers and digital technology during the 1970s, 1980s and 1990s.

One notable source of inspiration is the work of Ivan Illich himself. Indeed, in later life, Illich reportedly used a personal computer extensively and was often frustrated that it was technically not possible for him to reprogram its operating system or core software applications to fit his personal needs (Samerski 2018). In this sense, Illich was keenly aware of the computer's enormous power alongside its devastating effects on his body, senses and social interactions. On this latter point, Illich described the computer as a 'mindboggling' device – a tool that stops people thinking for themselves, that demands they rely on technology rather than their own senses to tell them what they feel and what they are.

Yet, rather than being anti-computer, Illich was interested in thinking about how digital technologies could be used in appropriate, circumspect and collective ways. He saw this as requiring continual awareness of the limitations of using digital environments for supporting communication, knowledge building and the development of a collective subjectivity. Indeed, Illich talked about the need for people to cultivate a 'technological ascesis'

The Case for Digital Degrowth 65

– a critical distancing that allows one to reflect on the extent to which one is engaged in responsible use of digital technology, and when limits need to be applied. In this sense, Illich could see how computer use might fit with his idea of tools for conviviality. For example, he remained enthusiastic about the potential of networking. As Marco Deriu recounts: 'Illich identifies computer networks and the ability to create connections between peer groups based on similar interests in the same city, or even in distant lands, as an alternative means of meeting, creating and having social relationships' (2015: 80).

Illich's early forays with a PC offer a lively reminder of the value of 1980s' computer culture. This was a time when the encroachment of computers into everyday life was not taken as inevitable, and the idea of people exerting control over their relationships with new technology was deemed worthy of serious consideration. Indeed, alongside prominent names such as Illich, many of the early computing movements of the 1970s and 1980s were open to similar lines of thinking around how this new area of technology might play out. In some ways, the notion of digital degrowth chimes with the early days of computing technology, when 'microcomputing' was primarily the preserve of individual hobbyists and enthusiastic amateurs who spent considerable amounts of time building and adapting their own hardware, writing and sharing their own programs, and pursuing computing as an experimental grassroots activity.

For example, in his history of the origins of computing, Steven Levy (1984) describes how some of the early hobbyist pioneers were directly inspired by Illich's writing. This was evident in widely shared enthusiasms for open-source and public-access principles, as well as advancing computing through loosely organized non-hierarchical clubs where like-minded people could come together to learn about the new technology, lend each other resources, give advice, 'tinker' and collectively develop the technology. Tellingly, these early stages of pre-Big Tech computing were also notably ecologically minded. As Morell notes, 'environmentalism and ecology were important inspirations – present in the [early] language, terminology and ecosystemic thinking of internet communities' (2015: 159). Similarly, the early development of the worldwide web was also notably driven by collectivist and commons-based ambitions (Berners-Lee 2010). When seen through the lens of these computing pioneers, the idea of

66 Digital Degrowth

digital degrowth certainly seems familiar and feasible. There is much to be said for recapturing and reanimating this passion, enthusiasm, expertise, ingenuity and – above all – the underpinning ethos of computing as a collective pursuit rather than a commercial enterprise.

Looking beyond the Global North

Of course, any push for digital degrowth needs to be more than a revival of ideas from a narrow set of middle-aged white men 'tinkering' with computers fifty years ago in North America and Europe. Regardless of their social awareness and eco-ambitions, the computer hobbyists of the 1970s and 1980s arguably laid the foundations for much that is wrong with current forms of digital excess. As argued in Chapter 3, it is well worth also looking further afield for precedents, not least to Global South communities and contexts whose engagements with digital technologies have long been substantially constrained by climate, hostile environments, limited resources and intermittent infrastructure. In short, when looking for precedents for any new notion of digital degrowth, it is worth considering what can be learnt from the forms of digital technology that have developed (and sometimes flourished) in countries, regions and contexts whose needs have long been compromised and marginalized due to resource constraints and hostile environments.

Various regions in West and East Africa certainly provide ample illustration of what scaled-back and slowed-down forms of technology engagement can look like. These forms of computing are shaped by several contextual constraints, including intermittent and unreliable power supplies, limited access to devices, the difficulties of maintaining them, and the general fragility of digital technology resources in the face of harsh environmental conditions. Many of these contexts are also hampered by the problem of poor (or non-existent) 'last mile' internet connectivity, i.e. the final portion of the telecommunications network chain that physically connects the end-user with main trunklines. In the face of these challenges, various practical responses have emerged across African communities, not least the ongoing work in the areas of 'alternative technology' and 'intermediate technology', as well as the 'ecotechnology' and 'ICT for development'

The Case for Digital Degrowth 67

(ICT4D) movements. All these approaches offer valuable understandings and insights that have direct relevance to rethinking the use of digital technology.

For example, in terms of appropriate forms of digital technology, innovations include the design and production of low-cost and low-energy devices designed to be dust and water resistant. These can take the form of devices powered by wind-up and hand-cranked generators as well as solar power. Alongside these is the enduring tradition of community access points, from internet kiosks through to device libraries and other forms of shared access to devices. Also of interest are the different iterations of local cultures of repair and maintenance that persist in low-income locations with limited access to technology. These include small family-run 'tech shops', mobile phone repairers and even large repair markets – many of which are aligned with local repair cultures relating to vehicles, tyres, household appliances and similar.

Work in the field of ICT4D also points to various types of digital hardware and infrastructure that support resilient forms of technology use in resource-constrained environments. Alongside the continued use of physical storage mediums such as USB sticks, CD-ROMs and external hard drives, this has also seen the development of online services that convert bandwidth intensive content into more accessible low-data content, thereby allowing users without broadband connections to access digital content. Also of interest are various alternative sources of internet connectivity, from cooperative computer networks that run improvised wireless networks, through to ways of ensuring 'last mile' internet connectivity (for example, allowing local internet connections through spare television broadcasting bandwidth). Finally, a range of alternate off-grid electricity approaches are being pursued to address issues of power generation, including cheap photovoltaic solar panels, local micro-grids and the increased use of lithium batteries to store energy.

These are all useful starting points for reflecting on the unsustainable cultural understandings and assumptions that have built up around Global North forms of digital technology use over the past forty years. Indeed, the forms of technology use that have thrived most in low-income contexts contrast sharply with the tendency in Global North regions to develop digital technology in fundamentally unconstrained and profligate ways. In comparison

68 Digital Degrowth

to expecting high-spec and always-on ways of operating, the forms of digital practice just outlined demonstrate ways in which digital technologies can be conceived around the frailties of infrastructures that need to be maintained and cared for, rather than continually improved and upgraded. As Steve Jackson and colleagues note in terms of local maintenance and repair cultures in East Africa, the Global North has much to learn from 'the distinctively different worlds of design and practice that appear to us when we take erosion, breakdown, and decay ("broken world thinking") rather than novelty, growth, and progress as our starting point' (2012: 107).

The idea of 'radically sustainable technology'

Finally, there are also plenty of degrowth-adjacent ideas emerging within the margins of computer science, software development and digital activist communities – what the Finnish computer artist Ville-Matias Heikkilä (2021) describes as forms of 'radically sustainable computing'. While not developed under the banner of degrowth per se, these approaches certainly provide various examples of how computing can be decoupled from the growth-focused imperatives of capitalist society. To date, such efforts have progressed in a piecemeal manner, led by disparate groups with broad interests in alternate approaches to digital technology. The hope, of course, is that these initial developments might signal the beginnings of mainstream change.

One area of interest involves what has been labelled 'collapse informatics'. This emphasizes the importance of 'preparedness' approaches to computing, i.e. building systems in the abundant present that might later prove durable during times of scarcity. Such efforts chime with the 'Computing Within Limits' (LIMITS) community of academics, software developers and activists. LIMITS sets out to reimagine the development of digital technology through principles of constraint and restraint. This stresses the need to develop forms of computing that fit with rapidly changing real-world environmental limits (Pargman and Wallsten 2017), therefore rejecting 'cornucopian' presumptions of limitless, replicable technology resources. Instead, LIMITS pushes for radically leaner and ecologically aware approaches to developing and deploying digital technology across societies.

The Case for Digital Degrowth

Allied to this is the notion of 'permacomputing', advocating the application of permaculture principles to the digital domain. Here, interests centre on developing ways in which computing can be sustained through practices of reuse, repair, maintenance and non-waste. Crucially, permacomputing stresses the development of digital technologies that are drastically less reliant on artificial energy, and designed in ways that acknowledge their interdependence with natural systems. As Mike Grindle (2023) puts it: 'just as permaculture seeks to empower resilient and regenerative practices in agriculture, permacomputing hopes to do the same in the technological sector'.

Elsewhere, picking up on the success of the 'slow food' movement, a philosophy of 'slow computing' has been developed as a practical alternative to the accelerated digital lifestyles fuelled by commercial data extraction. As Rob Kitchin and Alistair Fraser put it, this is an effort to 'experience the joy of computing – to continue to use digital technologies for all kinds of productive purposes – while also reining in some of the more problematic aspects of living digital lives' (2020: 168). Slow principles can therefore be applied to any aspect of the digital ecosystem, pushing for forms of 'capital switching' where resources are switched from goals of global growth and value extraction to goals of care and local sufficiency. For example, the idea of a 'slow data economy' offers an alternative to the unregulated and rampantly expansionist business models and processes of data-driven markets such as cryptocurrencies, geofencing and generative AI. This involves the responsible development of digital technologies along the line of social innovation, prioritizing the creation of social value, the maintenance of existing infrastructure, and a focus on local, place-based approaches that are not intended to scale (Crampton 2024).

Alongside these burgeoning movements is the idea of 'digital sufficiency'. This marks a deliberate move away from mainstream calls (outlined in Chapter 2) for the 'greening' of digital technology and efforts to prolong digital technology growth along the lines of consistency ('doing things better') and efficiency ('doing more with less'). In contrast, digital sufficiency pushes for the absolute reduction of resource and energy demands in ways that maintain (or even improve) general living conditions and perhaps widen opportunities for everyone to lead flourishing lives. As such, digital sufficiency implies a rethinking of digital technology along appropriately refined lines of frugality, slow consumption, downshifting and minimalism.

More specifically, Santarius et al. (2023) suggest that the idea of digital sufficiency can be seen in terms of four different dimensions. First is the principle of 'hardware sufficiency'. This calls for societies where fewer digital devices are produced and consumed. Any newly produced devices should be designed along robust and durable lines, resulting in long-lasting computer hardware that keeps absolute energy demands to the lowest levels possible while remaining capable of performing the required tasks. Deliberate efforts are made to ensure that the complexity and resource use of any device does not surpass the core purposes it is designed for. This ideal of sufficient (rather than superfluous) computing power is therefore analogous to the maxim of 'not using a sledgehammer to crack a nut'.

Second is the principle of 'software sufficiency'. This involves working out ways to design and develop software products that avoid non-essential data transfer, require minimal amounts of processing power and energy drain, and generally make the smallest possible demands on computer hardware. In practical terms, this might involve the design of software products that do not facilitate any transfer of data other than is strictly necessary for the core functionality of the product. Software might be designed to be run offline as often as possible, and/or not transfer data automatically to third parties.

The third principle is 'user sufficiency', i.e. the idea of using digital technologies as frugally as possible, in ways that promote sustainable lifestyles and support a decent quality of living. Such ideals might be achieved in several ways. For example, people can be encouraged to embrace the idea of the working life of digital technologies being extended through practices of maintenance and repair. This might also see the development of community-wide opportunities to share devices and acquire pre-used technologies. People can also be encouraged to reflect on their habitual patterns of device (over)use. This might also involve IT providers being required to publicize the environmental harms associated with their products – such as device manufacturers publishing 'ingredient lists' of the resources and origins of their hardware products, or software providers including live notifications of the carbon emissions accruing from any software and system use.

Finally, there is the challenge of 'economic sufficiency'. This involves reorienting IT production to remain within bounds that do not pose a threat to planetary well-being. Here, it is argued that governments need to ban blatantly environmentally harmful forms of IT such as cryptocurrency mining. Elsewhere, Santarius et al. (2023) suggest concerted efforts to 'decommercialize the internet' – discouraging or disrupting third-party data scraping practices, enacting advertising bans to disrupt the profitability of the data brokering industry, and similar actions intended to decouple technology use from economic growth.

Toward a sense of digital degrowth

All these precedents certainly offer strong foundations on which to progress our own ideas of digital degrowth. That said, nothing outlined in the previous sections provides a completely neat, wholly unproblematic blueprint for moving forward. For example, digital degrowth cannot simply be a revival of the spirit of the early computer pioneers of the 1970s and 1980s. While much is made of the countercultural origins of 'homebrew computing', the politics of these pioneers was often at odds with the collectivist, ecojustice orientations of degrowth thinking. This pre-Silicon Valley culture was notably deficient in terms of its inclusivity (especially in terms of the gender, race and age of its participants), and its interest in technical rather than social issues (Turner 2006). Moreover, the 'Californian ideology' that drove the progress of computing in the US was an awkward combination of the self-sustainable development of computing technology with a strand of cyber-libertarianism that now persists in the dangerous pronouncements and reckless actions of the likes of Marc Andreessen, Elon Musk, Peter Thiel and other Silicon Valley luminaries (Golumbia 2024).

Similarly, we need to be wary of a romantic re-Orientalist 'othering' of technology practices in middle-income and low-income countries – seizing on these low-tech approaches as exotic solutions to be seamlessly appropriated by those in the Global North. Conversely, there is also a danger of slipping into an unhelpful apocalyptic mindset. For example, ideas around collapse informatics do not imply an extreme survivalist form of technology – what might be characterized as a 'prepper' version of digital technology. Nevertheless, all these different approaches do offer glimpses into what scaled-back, slowed-down, self-determined forms of digital technology might look like. Crucially, these are visions and versions of digital technology that are decoupled from the capitalist imperatives of extractive and exploitative economic growth, as well as the relentless accumulation of capital. These are forms of technology that are not under the direct control of big business or authoritative state dictates; they are mindful of energy limitations and resource constraints, and fit with degrowth ambitions of doing 'more with less'. There is much in the ideas of permacomputing, digital sufficiency and technological ascesis that can be taken forward into our own envisioning of digital degrowth.

All these precedents point to two complementary lines along which degrowth principles can be used to reframe digital technology in low-impact and equitable terms. On the one hand there is the need for clarity on what sorts of digital technology our societies might want less of and/or none of. Indeed, everything discussed so far in this book highlights the pressing need to identify technologies that are wholly irredeemable in any degrowth society, i.e. technologies that need to be rejected outright because they are 'destructive no matter who owns them' (Illich 1973: 26). These might include genetically modified organisms, nuclear power and nanotechnologies, alongside digital developments such as cryptocurrencies, non-fungible tokens and other digital innovations that are entwined with efforts to stimulate economic growth while also incurring environmentally reckless levels of energy consumption.

At the same time, these alternative approaches also highlight the need to call out and resist resource intensive and/or socially harmful digital technologies that are unlikely to change their ways – technologies 'that cannot be made sustainable, contribute little use values, or are superfluous consumption' (Schmelzer, Vetter and Vansintjan 2022: 9). These are the digital technologies that need to be downscaled and eventually phased out altogether in the transition to a more sustainable future. They include online advertising and data brokering, but we might also call out forms of digital technology built around predatory IT industry practices such as planned obsolescence, 'free-mium' pricing strategies, gamification and other manipulative business tactics. Alongside these blatantly egregious products are many other technology

The Case for Digital Degrowth 73

uses that might appear more benign but are equally superfluous and/or of little added value. For example, if we are being honest, how essential is it for most people to make live video calls or upload endless live-streamed high-definition video? When one stops to think about it, there are countless forms of digital technology that are not worth the environmental and social harms that are incurred through their use.

The next important question to ask is what forms of digital technology we might consider worth keeping in support of the transition to a degrowth society. Indeed, everything discussed over the past two chapters points to the need for clarity on what sorts of digital technology we *do* want. This might take two forms. First there are the existing convivial forms of digital technology that we might want more of – those that can be maintained by local communities and be adopted and adapted in ways that lead to expanded freedoms, creativity, autonomy and happiness. These would be digital technologies that people can take management of and exercise direct democratic control over; technologies that are 'acceptable up to certain limits, which should be deliberated by the whole of society' (Flipo and Schneider 2015: xxv).

Existing digital technologies might be re-evaluated in terms of where they can realistically be expected to support broader degrowth actions. This might include digital technologies that contribute to the reduction of less necessary production and the scaling down of destructive economic sectors. It would also include digital technologies that clearly improve people's experiences of public services and go some way to ensuring universal access to high-quality education, healthcare and housing, or that support wider efforts to reduce people's working time, or increase their capacity to work part-time or in 'green jobs'.

Second, and perhaps most exciting, is the need to stimulate development of completely new convivial digital technologies that can play a part in supporting degrowth transitions, encouraging forms of digital innovation that foster principles of conviviality, commoning and care, dematerialization and self-sufficiency. As has been stressed throughout the past two chapters, any transition to degrowth will arguably require more innovation and novel technology development – pushing technology developers and designers to reappraise most of the fundamental preconceptions they have about 'new' technology. This involves the

74   Digital Degrowth

design challenge of developing digital technologies that use as few resources as possible and that are easy to implement, easy to use and easy to maintain. It also involves rethinking the very form and nature of what digital technologies are, from the materials they are physically constructed from and the energy sources they draw upon, through to the ways in which they interact with their local environments. Most importantly, it involves reconsidering the 'how' and 'why' of what these technologies can help people and communities to do – in other words, what new forms of social relations and practices, political dynamics, societal and environmental outcomes they can be designed to support. As we shall see in Chapters 5 and 6, degrowth thinking pushes the idea of future digital innovation in radically different and considerably more earth-bound directions.

Conclusions

The next two chapters go on to sketch out what these various forms of digital degrowth might look like – from the most immediate changes that our communities and societies can make, through to ambitious longer-term reimaginings of the 'digital technology' we might want to come to fruition in a few decades' time. As this chapter has outlined, there are plenty of reasons to be hopeful, and plenty of already existing forms of digital technology that are sustainable, equitable and dignified. So, we now need to make connections between all the ideas and ideals outlined across this chapter. What forms of digital technology might genuinely support wider degrowth transitions toward more socially beneficial ways of living and the scaling back of environmentally harmful industries? How can we develop a shared collective critical consciousness when it comes to deciding which digital technologies are not welcome in our local communities and wider societies? How can we manufacture durable, rugged and repairable forms of digital hardware that can withstand harsh environmental conditions and compromised connectivity? How do we encourage popular understandings of digital technology as something that has clearly defined limits associated with its interdependence with natural systems?

The next two chapters explore how all these concerns can stimulate a sense of doing digital technology differently: rethinking, as Jason Hickel (2023) puts it, 'how technology is imagined and the conditions under which it is deployed'. This implies forms of digital technology that are fit for times of societal and ecological instability and that intrinsically support degrowth transitions. To return to a point from previous chapters, degrowth is not anti-technology per se, but is opposed to any form of technology that is harmful and excessive. In this sense, degrowth challenges us to rethink the nature of what we understand digital innovation to be in the current era. With all these thoughts in mind, let us now start considering what a vision of digital degrowth might look like.

5
Finding Alternatives in the Here and Now

Introduction

So, what might digital degrowth look like in practice? How might these concerns be enacted in ways that begin to initiate meaningful change? This chapter considers the first two challenges set out in Chapter 4: (i) how we might *oppose* current forms of digital technology that are clearly irredeemable to human and environmental flourishing; and (ii) how we can *support* existing forms of digital technology that are clearly conducive to degrowth ambitions. As Jathan Sadowski (2025) contends, any attempt to move beyond digital capitalism needs to work out which digital technologies 'should be taken apart, to be rebuilt for new purposes', as well as which simply need to be 'destroyed for good'. As such, this chapter highlights various ideas that can be actioned immediately – practices, processes and technologies that already exist on the sidelines of mainstream digital technology. These are alternatives that are already well within our grasp, what White and Williams describe as 'non-capitalist practices already used and preferred in the here and now' (2016: 330).

This chapter offers some starting points for rethinking digital technology in ways that are socially just, ecologically sustainable and better aligned with the needs of people and the planet.

Crucially, these are all ways to support technology development that is decoupled from the capitalist logic of endless expansion, extraction and growth. They are all illustrations of how people can work collectively to refashion digital technology in ways that are locally determined, resulting in technology use that promotes sociability rather than individuality. While some of these examples might seem modest, especially in comparison to the bombast of Big Tech marketing, they are all notable for their underpinning character and values. They are actions and alterations that can be enacted on the margins, creating initial 'cracks' and opening spaces where dominant forms of digitization might begin to be deconstructed (Feola 2019), and where we might advance digitally informed ways of living that are more open, communal, sharable, repairable, controllable and, ultimately, fairer. Here, then, are some examples of what such changes might initially entail.

Opposing 'irredeemable' ways of doing technology

The first challenge is getting rid of current forms of digital technology that are irredeemable to degrowth – instances of digital excess that need to be rejected outright because they are fundamentally harmful in whatever form they exist. This opposition can take place in different ways, through democratic deliberation and collective action as well as through direct protest and agitation. Regardless of nature and intent, these actions will only be successful if accompanied by public willingness for change. All these proposals mean very little unless people have a good understanding of digital degrowth and are generally supportive of such changes. In the short term, at least, digital degrowth will be as much a matter of changing people's minds as changing digital practices.

(i) Influencing public opinion and political thinking

Any moves toward digital degrowth will first require a collective reset of how people understand and engage with digital technology – establishing a popular consensus that current modes of digital excess and over-consumption are no longer acceptable in relation to how we want to live. While this might seem unthinkable when set against the recent hegemony of Google, Meta and other Big Tech corporations, history shows that societies are well capable of moving on from human activities that are habitual but harmful. For example, European societies no longer support the transatlantic slave trade, child labour or denying women the right to vote. More recently, after forty years of vehement mainstream climate denial, opinion now seems to be finally edging toward a collective acceptance that living in a world dependent on the burning of fossil fuels is not sustainable. Significant societal changes that at one point would have seemed completely unthinkable (if not wholly unwarranted) can, then, steadily become the norm. In light of all these other transitions, advancing societies on from a few decades of digital excess is surely achievable.

Indeed, this task of chipping away at the current digital orthodoxy is perhaps comparable to ongoing efforts in some countries to move away from car culture. While it might have previously seemed unimaginable, public appetite is now growing for restricting the sale of gasoline vehicles and redirecting public money toward public transport infrastructure and car-free zones in towns and cities. All this comes after Western lifestyles and built environments had been fundamentally shaped around the automobile for much of the twentieth century. Now, despite fierce opposition from the automobile and oil industries, the tide seems to be starting to turn. As with car culture, we need to begin promoting the idea that the digital age is just another passing phase in human history and one equally subject to 'the obvious axiom that nothing can grow indefinitely' (Kallis et al. 2020: 11). All of this requires sustained campaigns of public information and publicity designed to reform commonsense understandings around excessive digital technology use. In thirty years' time, the idea of owning multiple digital devices will hopefully seem as abhorrent as owning multiple SUVs, and the idea of building new data centres as environmentally reckless as building coal-fuelled power stations.

Such shifts in public opinion and political thinking will require sustained publicity strategies to occupy mainstream discussions and debates around digital technology. One key focus will be public denouncement – calling out digital harms and altering mainstream conversations around the impacts of digital technology on everyday life and society. This will include debunking the messages pushed through tech industry advertising, and 'resist[ing] false solutions, such as so-called innovative "smart", "green" and "sustainable" technologies, vocally and in print' (Liegey and Nelson 2020: 68). At the same time, public support for digital degrowth is most likely to flourish through positive messaging. As Birte Strunk (2023) reminds us, degrowth is a dialectic that can be framed both as 'a threat to be overcome' and 'a promise to be fulfilled'. In this latter sense, digital degrowth ideas such as voluntary simplicity and 'right to repair' are in tune with wider shifts in societal thinking around how we might best live our lives along sustainable and manageable lines. It is important that the positive qualities of slowed-down and scaled-back modes of digital living become part of mainstream public and political conversations.

(ii) *Making the digital technology a focus of deliberative democracy*

Public views around digital degrowth can also be refined through the growing appetite for citizen assemblies, citizen councils, citizen juries and other forms of deliberative democracy. These involve groups of people (carefully selected as representative of wider populations) coming together regularly to deliberate on matters of importance. These 'mini publics' are supported by experts and scientific advice, and work toward developing informed decisions which are then presented to governments, officials and other authorities. The thoroughness of this process, and the emphasis placed on public-wide representation, means that citizen assembly decisions usually attract high levels of attention, are seen to be highly legitimate, and play an important role in shaping public moods around matters of importance.

The past few years have seen a succession of high-profile citizen assemblies set up to deliberate on various aspects of climate change mitigation. Crucially, a spate of recent national assemblies across Europe has demonstrated public opinions on these issues to be remarkably bold. For example, these assemblies were considerably more willing (sometimes by a factor of six) than their governments to make recommendations about sufficiency and to insist on absolute reductions in production and consumption (Lage et al. 2023). The French 'Convention Citoyenne pour le Climat' resulted in a 460-page document with 149 policy

80 Digital Degrowth

proposals, including calls to prohibit planned obsolescence, ban advertising for carbon intensive items, and place strict limits on overpackaging and single-use plastics.

There is clear sense in getting digital issues included in future programmes of deliberative democracy, either as part of established citizen assemblies on climate change mitigation, or perhaps as a completely new strand of citizen assembly work. This could include citizen assemblies focused on developing recommendations for local community technology change rather than working to influence state and parliamentary politics (Ejsing, Veng and Papazu 2023). Even democratizing the procurement of digital technologies in local institutions such as schools, libraries, government services and other workplaces can begin to get people comfortable with the idea of deciding collectively which digital technologies are genuinely beneficial, and which uses need to be curtailed. Digital degrowth is based on the principle of local communities collectively deciding what forms of digital technology they agree are desirable. Any mechanism through which people can begin to get a taste of 'deciding for ourselves' will be a valuable step toward such autonomy.

(iii) Organizing protest and resistance

Alongside deliberation and persuasion, there is also room for approaches that directly confront and resist the most egregious aspects of digital excess. Digital degrowth certainly chimes with recent high-profile protests and campaigns against large-scale government and corporate forms of technology implementation. For example, the past few years have seen vocal push-back against facial recognition technology from civil liberties and human rights groups alongside consumer organizations and trade unions. Similar campaigns have been waged against the impact of AI and online gig-work on employment conditions and worker rights. Spurred by the direct action of climate groups such as Extinction Rebellion and Earth First!, we are now seeing calls for forms of 'neo-Luddite sabotage' as a tool for directly disrupting the most harmful aspects of digital capitalism and reclaiming 'the multitude's role in shaping the technological commons of their general intellect' (Carter and Yang 2023: 366). Elsewhere, while perhaps animated by more reactionary-minded concerns, there have also been popular campaigns to restrict the reach of social media platforms and to establish public spaces as 'smartphone-free'. With popular sentiment growing around the impact of digital technologies on the quality of people's lives, well-directed campaigns and protests against digital excess will likely find popular support around the world.

While such activities are usually aimed at lobbying government and state regulators, a key part of digital degrowth will be direct local actions. These would follow the lead recently set by organized community resistance against some of the worst local instances of Big Tech-driven environmental harms. For example, protesting and organized resistance has been particularly successful in drought-ridden regions faced with the imposition of data centres and IT manufacturing hubs. The past few years have seen organized resistance to lithium mining in Indigenous communities in Nevada and in various parts of Spain. In the Acacoyagua region of Mexico, where 20 per cent of the territory was under mining concessions, local groups successfully organized protests, blockading and eventually halting operations (Ciacci 2023). In Chile, there has also been a spate of community fightbacks against the planned construction of Google data centres (Ramírez 2023). In Chihuahua, Mexico, local farmers have repeatedly occupied key dams in an effort to protect local community access to water. All these actions illustrate how 'a common sense of struggle' might be built up against Big Tech and the machinations of digital capitalism (Quijano 2023: 96). These are popular movements that align closely with digital degrowth sentiments.

(iv) Harnessing the efforts of tech workers

Another strategy to actively advance digital degrowth goals will be harnessing the efforts of tech industry workers. As noted in Chapter 4, digital degrowth is not an idealistic call for the immediate shutdown of the IT industry. On the contrary, it is important to acknowledge that any transition toward digital degrowth will realistically require the continuation of for-profit tech companies (at least in the short to mid-term). This means that tech workers can play important roles in shifting the values and logics that drive their companies' actions and agendas. In this sense, digital degrowth changes might well be possible from *within* Big Tech corporations, through initiatives led by the IT professionals that these corporations employ.

82 Digital Degrowth

Such actions might take a couple of forms. Most obvious is tech workers directly pushing their employers to engage in more societally and environmentally beneficial work. They can demand more say in the types of technology they are involved in developing. Those in management and decision-making positions can encourage a focus on the work of maintenance and repair. They can also subtly promote cultures of organizational downscaling, making decisions during the course of their work that slow down and dilute corporate ambitions to get involved in every sector of society and facet of everyday life.

At the same time, however, digital degrowth requires the building of technical expertise and know-how within local communities, boosting their capacity to 'do technology for themselves'. In this context, tech industry employees might also push to be redeployed to roles within local and community tech initiatives. This might be achieved through community volunteering and secondments that allow tech workers to support their own local communities, or perhaps even the formation of tech-focused 'peace corps' to support regions that lack high numbers of tech-savvy citizens. Given that any transition to digital degrowth will require high levels of technological expertise, it will be important to build allies within the tech industry and redirect the efforts of its workforce in every way possible.

The idea of tech workers acting as allies of digital degrowth is not as far-fetched as it might sound. Indeed, some tech workers are already taking moral and ethical leads on pushing the IT industry to work for better forms of digital technology and better forms of contemporary society. As Robert Dorschel (2022) has argued, a surprising number of tech workers (at least those in programming, development and other creative positions) seem ready to push for tech-related outcomes that are more socially fair, less harmful and generally more progressive than at present. The past few years have seen spates of employee activism and push-back from within Big Tech corporations against contracted work in defence, national security and law enforcement sectors (Ahmed 2024). Any shift to digital degrowth will be bolstered by strong buy-in from these factions of the tech community.

(v) Encouraging the 'redesigning' and 'undesigning' of technologies

It is also worth considering how tech designers and the wider design community can be engaged in work that pushes back against undesirable forms of technology. This could involve technology designers and developers taking on socially focused 'undesign' briefs – what James Pierce (2012) describes as 'negating technology by design'. This would involve tech designers working to eliminate technologies that are agreed to be wholly destructive and harmful to the collective good; in short, working to design egregious hardware and software out of existence. It might be possible, for example, to design computer servers that function in ways that significantly restrict or completely disrupt wasteful digital practices – what Pierce refers to as designed erasure. Alternatively, technology designers and developers might also work to introduce limitations and constraints on generally undesirable technologies – imposing caps on data use, deaccelerating processing speeds, and generally restricting technology consumption to sustainable and acceptable levels. Pierce refers to this as designed inhibition, i.e. designs that aim to hinder or prevent the use of technology in particular ways that are considered harmful and in contexts that are especially vulnerable to these harms.

Alongside these shifts is what Cameron Tonkinwise (2018) terms 'de-progressive design' – technology designers and developers working to rediscover and reclaim past ways of doing things that have been discarded in the relentless forward-focused expansion of digital technologies. This could involve the revitalization of 'standalone' digital products that are not networked to mainstream energy sources or cloud computing. It might also involve developing new versions of older analogue products and processes that are considerably less resource intensive and socially harmful than their digital equivalents. All told, technology development and design can be reimagined as a process of slowing down and defanging the digital excesses of the past few decades. Rather than being put out of job, a transition to digital degrowth will mean that there is plenty of work for technology designers to be getting on with.

Supporting 'desirable' ways of doing technology

While these moves to undo irredeemable technologies are important initial steps, ultimately digital degrowth is a positive push for a transition to a new regime of digital technology. In this sense, we need also to consider ways of bolstering existing forms of digital technology that might be considered complementary to degrowth goals. In contrast to the many digital technologies that might well be irredeemable, there are many examples of better digital technologies, practices and protocols that currently exist on the margins of digital culture and consumerism. The challenge here is working out ways to advance these existing forms of digital technology in ways that lead to expanded freedom, creativity, autonomy and happiness. Pushing these forms of digital technology forward is therefore an important step toward digital degrowth.

(i) Digital public goods and the digital commons

Most obvious in this context is the computing that has been developed over the past forty years around 'open' principles. In contrast to closed forms of proprietary for-profit technology, these are forms of digital technology where software, standards and hardware designs are open to all, knowledge is freely shared and collectively refined, and technology development is driven by motivations of collective endeavour rather than individual gain. An obvious initial step in advancing digital degrowth will therefore be encouraging a mass turn toward ideas such as free software, open source, open data, open standards and other models of computing that embody the idea of digital public goods.

All these examples offer strong starting points for developing digital software and hardware that is collectively developed and maintained for the good of society rather than commercial gain. These are digital technologies that can be made freely available to everyone in ways that are non-excludable. These forms of computing clearly correspond with degrowth principles of the commons – reorienting digital technology as a 'gift economy' where 'property is freely given away, there is no accumulation, no money or other medium of exchange, and no exchange value' (Fuchs 2008: 162). These are digital systems that are defiantly non-proprietary in nature, developed through the collaborative sharing of resources amongst wide networks of like-minded people around the world.

Key here will be the use of these technologies with clear political intent. In the past, free and open approaches to computing and technology development have proven prone to capture by neoliberal and ultra-libertarian values. As Langdon Winner (1997) warns, while often claiming a political agnosticism, enthusiasm for 'free' and 'open' digital movements is sometimes motivated by 'radical, right-wing libertarian ideas about the proper definition of freedom, social life, economics, and politics'. In contrast, then, digital degrowth will involve the revitalization of open computing movements along deliberately communitarian, ecojustice and post-capitalist lines. Toward the end of his life, André Gorz came to firmly believe that open-source tools could easily be reclaimed along collectivist lines to support self-production and allow people to collectively decide ways of living, producing, and consuming (Kerschner et al. 2018). As Gorz put it, 'the struggle between open source and proprietary software has been at the crux of the key conflict defining our times. The conflict extends and prolongs itself into the struggle against the commercialization of our primary assets and resources' (cited in Fourel and Corpet 2012).

Reorienting mainstream digital technology around such principles would ensure a far-reaching and powerful digital culture. Current mainstream open-source packages include the Linux operating system, the Firefox web browser, the OpenOffice suite of 'office' applications, and the Apache web server. Perhaps the most established example of a digital commons is the online encyclopaedia Wikipedia, one of the largest, most recognizable and widely used reference resources of current times. Wikipedia exists in an open format where users can create, amend and delete entries and information as they feel fit. Crucially, people are free to download the entire Wikipedia database and distribute it offline to those without internet connectivity. There is also interest in how open knowledge networks can be used to support local degrowth efforts to share knowledge, expertise and software resources on a global basis, allowing local actions to gain a wider momentum. Vasilis Kostakis (2024) describes how digital communication networks can be used to connect local Makerspaces and Fab-Labs to engage in 'locally oriented but

86 Digital Degrowth

globally connected' small manufacturing ventures – sharing digital design files, software and knowledge via online networks that constitute a 'global digital commons'. Kostakis, Pazaitis and Liarokapis (2023) describe this amplification of low-tech local actions through high-tech telecommunications as 'mid-tech' – leveraging the benefits of high-tech networking where it can be of social benefit to all with minimal environmental harm.

(ii) Building our own computers

The spirit of open computing communities extends to the development of computing hardware. Digital degrowth will also involve the expansion of alternative hardware cultures where devices are constructed in utilitarian and refined ways. As highlighted in earlier chapters, the current design and manufacture of digital devices are trapped in a cycle of over-specification. For example, smartphones are now over-fitted with multiple cameras, while gaming PCs are designed to consume vastly higher amounts of energy than conventional computers. None of this digital excess can be deemed necessary, especially when powerful computing hardware can be produced in much simpler and less resource intensive ways. One good example is minicomputers and single-board computers – tiny devices with a few microchips, processors and other basic components crammed onto small circuit boards to provide basic computing capabilities at much lower cost and lower environmental impact than standard devices.

One highly successful example of the single-board computer is the Raspberry Pi. Launched at the beginning of the 2010s, the Raspberry Pi has since thrived, with improved models being developed on a regular basis and large communities of enthusiasts forming to share ideas, hacks and open-source code. Originally intended as a cheap way of teaching children about the basics of computing, it is estimated that well over 30 million Raspberry Pi units were sold within the first ten years, with the device retailing for as little as $35. Crucially, Raspberry Pi boards have been taken up for all manner of real-world applications, with the devices proving capable of weather monitoring, allowing homeowners to check on their energy consumption, and powering various forms of control technology in industrial settings. Raspberry Pis have also been used to power smart speakers, digital cameras and FM radio broadcasting, to act as webservers and to run many

Finding Alternatives in the Here and Now

other computing applications that usually rely on much more resource-hungry digital hardware. Its rudimentary nature also means that a Raspberry Pi can connect with old hardware (such as printers and scanners) that are otherwise incompatible with present-day computers. The device has therefore been praised as an archetypal example of degrowth computing – a 'transitional, lesser computer' (Sutherland 2022) that still can function as a workstation.

Supporting the wider take up of single-board computers would be an obvious move in shifting mainstream digital culture toward degrowth principles, allowing people to continue using computers but along convivial, collective, minimalist and frugal lines. Tellingly, however, Raspberry Pi is also proving a salutary lesson in how capitalism seeks to ruthlessly co-opt and profit from any promising idea. In 2024 the Raspberry Pi Foundation floated on the London stock exchange for over $50 million, with one of its major investors declaring that 'we are very excited about both the commercial and social impact [Raspberry Pi] can continue to deliver in the future' (cited in Speed 2024). This initial public offering (IPO) was celebrated as establishing a market for single-board computers worth up to $21 billion. Under digital degrowth such commercial motives would be rendered redundant. The value of projects like the Raspberry Pi lies in their offering a convivial and less harmful form of computing for the masses, rather than yet another product to be commercially exploited.

(iii) The right to digital repair

Another aspect of contemporary digital culture that resonates with degrowth principles is the 'Right to Repair' movement. While not unique to digital products, the idea of repairable digital devices has taken off over the past few years as a social movement, through organizations such as 'Right to Repair Europe' and the US-based 'Repair Coalition' advocacy and lobbying group. These efforts are supported by online platforms such as iFixIt which coordinate knowledge sharing and the sale of replacement components and parts. In response, we are now seeing legislators in regions such as the EU, the UK and California move to discourage manufacturers from designing products with deliberately restrictive features that inhibit the reparability of products.

88   Digital Degrowth

As might be expected, the IT industry has actively lobbied against such changes, arguing that allowing a right to repair somehow stifles innovation and/or poses security risks. Nevertheless, the repair, reuse and refurbishment of digital devices would be an obvious focus for encouraging digital degrowth. One practical move would be to support the continued growth of community repair groups and collectives such as the Dutch-initiated repair café network, which has over 3,000 local groups worldwide. Here, local volunteers hold open repair sessions in community locations, allowing people to bring in broken devices and access the necessary tools and parts to fix them with help from the volunteers. This spirit of 'do it together' can be extended to establish the repair of digital devices as an act of commoning the tools, spaces, knowledge and skills required to repair and refurbish them. These local groups also function as sites of knowledge sharing around how best to repair and refurbish digital technologies, both on a local face-to-face basis and through the online sharing of information about successful repairs.

(iv) Modular devices

As well as supporting these communal sites of digital repair, digital degrowth would involve the manufacture of digital devices that are deliberately designed to be repairable with everyday tools. There would be open documentation about the design of devices and thriving marketplaces for parts, tools and manuals. Where possible, sustainable forms of 3D printing could be used to produce replacement parts. Software and apps would be designed to run on older devices and lower-spec systems. In short, the viable notion of a 'digital device for life' could be established, in direct opposition to current accepted IT industry practices of planned obsolescence, perpetual upgrades and other wasteful forms of digital over-consumption.

There are already tangible examples of such design principles in various modular and disassemblable devices that embody ethical and fair trade approaches. One prominent example is the Dutch 'Fairphone' modular smartphone, which is deliberately designed to be opened and disassembled as well as repaired with replaceable parts. Crucially, the production of these devices promises to minimize the use of conflict minerals and pay fair wages to suppliers and factory workers. The Fairphone certainly

Finding Alternatives in the Here and Now

comes with impressive ethical credentials. It is manufactured using Fairtrade certified gold, recycled plastic tin and ethically sourced aluminium. The device is claimed to be e-waste neutral, and whereever possible is shipped from its factories by train rather than air freight. Similar principles are driving interest in modular laptops such as the US-designed Framework laptop. These devices are also made from recycled materials wherever possible, and designed to be easily disassembled and for old parts to be repaired or upgraded.

Developments such as these show how degrowth principles might inform new ways of designing and producing digital devices. Nevertheless, while products like the Fairphone and Framework have all have sold relatively well, they are not viable long-term alternatives. By aping the basic form and function of standard consumer smartphones and laptops, these products only go a small way toward atoning for the environmental and social harms of device use. Moreover, to date many people have purchased and used Fairphones as a political statement – in this sense these devices have so far been most significant for the lifestyle movements that have built up around them, promoting discussions around what ethical IT consumption might be (Haucke 2018). Yet the principle of modularity could easily be taken up as a standard model for device design and production. Digital degrowth can extend these modular and disassembly principles and work toward developing completely new forms of computing devices that can last for decades and be distributed at minimal or no cost.

(v) Communal and shared resources

One way of subverting the unequal distribution of digital devices is to transition away from the commercial sale of digital technologies altogether and instead support commons-based approaches to shared digital devices. The idea of computers and digital devices as shared resources is not new. During the 1990s and 2000s shared computers were commonly accessed in public sites, with libraries, community centres, schools and other community spaces hosting computers, internet access, printing and other forms of digital access. Similarly, most towns and cities were home to small, independently run 'internet cafés'. While now less prevalent in high-income countries, these forms of public provision continue in many other parts of the world as important parts of the digital infrastructure. As part of a transition to digital degrowth, such arrangements can be revitalized on a widescale basis in higher-income regions as people feel the need to make less frequent use of computers and other digital devices.

Such principles can also be supported by the loaning of digital devices. At present, various community organizations, local charities and other welfare groups operate 'device loan libraries' where people are given short-term access to smartphones, tablets or computers with free data. While these schemes often tend to be run as social welfare, again there is no reason why such arrangements cannot be extended and expanded to whole communities as an alternative to owning 'personal' devices. Indeed, there are various thriving examples of how commons-based ownership of digital devices can work. For example, in Barcelona, the successful eReuse scheme involves each member first sharing a device for others to use. In return they receive reciprocal access to all other devices in the programme. The pool of shared devices is bolstered by second-hand devices donated to the eReuse community by business and public organizations. The scheme is managed collectively through a network of local autonomous eReuse centres, with volunteers working to refurbish and maintain devices, as well as distributing and tracking them as they are used by community members. Again, such actions chime with degrowth principles, and could be easily replicated through local initiatives that are developed and run all around the world.

(vi) Collectively maintained and run infrastructure

Alongside the ideal of communal devices there are many other examples of how digital infrastructure and services might be maintained and run along local collective and self-determined lines. At present, digital infrastructures such as the internet, data centres and platforms are imbued with logics of scalability and ambitions to sustain endless economic growth. One important element of digital degrowth is working to descale these current forms of 'big' digital infrastructure along what Pansera, Lloveras and Durrant (2024) term more 'sober' lines. In terms of the internet, for example, this might include local groups taking responsibility for the care and repair of the material digital infrastructure in their neighbourhoods – maintaining physical cables, antennae, cellular towers and exchange points. This can also involve downscaling infrastructure wherever possible – only continuing to run the smallest and lowest-impact data centres and redirecting the logic of network design and internet protocols away from assumptions of scalability and perpetual growth.

Illustrative of how digital infrastructure might be downscaled are the various successful instances of small-scale community-owned internet services. These provide internet access and technical support to members who in turn offer services on the network and collectively engage in governing how it is used. Such networks typically involve a few thousand people but can be expanded to cover larger communities. The NYC Mesh, for example, aims to grow into a decentralized network that covers all of New York City's five boroughs. More advanced still was the development of Catalonia's Guifi.net throughout the 2010s, which spread gradually to other autonomous communities in Spain and by 2021 boasted over 37,000 active nodes and over 70,000 km of wireless links.

Another example of deliberately convivial digital infrastructure is the platform cooperative movement (Scholz and Schneider 2016). This promotes the development of alternatives to commercial service platforms and apps such as Uber – platforms that link customers to services such as taxi rides, house cleaning, delivery services and other forms of gig-work. The key difference is that platform cooperatives are wholly owned and run by local groups of workers whose services are being offered for hire. In this way, the local workers get to decide their collective conditions of employment, such as pricing, timing and distribution of any work that is taken on. These platforms are built to promote values of fairness, working conditions and worker welfare rather than profiteering, network effects and an ambition to scale-up on a national or worldwide basis.

Platform cooperatives and community internet services therefore offer powerful and practical examples of how digital technologies can be more fairly arranged around values of autonomy, democratic control, cooperativism, sharing, openness and solidarity. These are degrowth-friendly instances of digital technologies being arranged through localized social movements that can be expanded and extended to become mainstream ways of approaching and organizing the digital. The key point with each of these examples is not primarily the sophistication of the

92 Digital Degrowth

technology, but the richness of the collective values and goals that underpin them. Efforts such as these demonstrate that relatively basic forms of technology use can result in powerful social outcomes.

Conclusions

All these examples – and the convivial, commons-based principles that they embody – are significant starting points from which to begin imagining the practicalities of digital degrowth. Running through all of them is the ethos of what Barbas Babtista (2020) describes as 'questioning technology by commonly owning it'. Indeed, key here is the idea of reframing the digital as a matter of collective responsibility. As Matthias Schmelzer and colleagues (2022) remind us, degrowth is something that needs to be mobilized at a local, collective level. While most of the examples outlined in this chapter are relatively small-scale, they are all important illustrations of what might be possible. Free software, community internet networks and repair cafés can be seen as 'nowtopias' – tangible alternatives that are already flourishing in the cracks of digital capitalism. They represent plausible alternatives to hyper-individualized forms of digital technology that can be used to challenge and agitate for change, establishing digital technology as a site of contestation and as ripe for reimagining through a different political lens.

As such, these examples of doing digital technology differently – and the principles that underpin them – do not constitute a comprehensive suite of alternate digital products and practices that can be quickly taken up on a worldwide basis. Rather, they are challenges to continue to think otherwise, to imagine other forms of computing, and to stimulate people and communities to begin to act along similar lines. In particular, they highlight the need to look beyond technological artefacts and focus more on the people and politics that lie behind them. As such, we should not lose sight of the work involved in ideologically reorienting technology to serve degrowth goals (Likavcan and Scholz-Wackerle 2018). For example, we must remain mindful that many of the technologies just highlighted can easily serve other ends – as evident in Raspberry Pi's $50 million IPO and the rampant libertarianism that drives some open-source communities.

Yet, if animated by different values and ideologies, the same devices and practices can play key roles in shifting digital technology toward degrowth ends. In many ways, the convivial potential of all the examples outlined in this chapter resides within the 'networks of actors, rationales, and narratives' (March 2018: 1702) that are brought together through the act of working out what alternative forms of computing might entail. Moreover, these slowed down, scaled back forms of computing lend themselves to radically different ways of living with and through digital technology. A community internet service generates locally based connections and collaborations, and can promote online cultures of mutual respect and obligation between people who are also likely to come across each other offline. The open design of software deters the worst aspects of proprietary and predatory software design, and strips technology use back to its essential features and actions. This is a more inclusive, more grounded form of computing for the people. As Hug March concludes, any sense of digital degrowth is 'not just a question of "what technologies" but "who produces, manages and controls them", "to whom" they benefit and "what" are the objectives they serve' (2018: 1703).

6

Future Innovations

Introduction

Having considered these initial moves toward digital degrowth, we can now look further ahead. This chapter addresses the third challenge set out in Chapter 4: how we might set about innovating *new* forms of digital technology that embody degrowth principles and ambitions for more scaled-back, slowed-down, socially just and environmentally sensitive ways of living. These are forms of digital technology that can support radically different social relations and practices, political dynamics and environmental impacts that align with transitions to a degrowth society. While the ideas in this chapter are certainly speculative, most already exist in one form or another. As we shall see, plenty of radical thinking can be found within computer science research, hacker communities and technology-minded eco-activism that aligns with degrowth sensibilities. These examples all offer glimpses of plausible and possible forms of future living with digital technology.

This chapter is intended to get us thinking about what substantial longer-term transitions might follow on from the more immediate shifts outlined in Chapter 5. As argued throughout this book, long-term reinvention of the digital is a wholly necessary part of digital degrowth. If we accept that excessive consumption of digital technologies cannot continue indefinitely, then it makes good sense to contemplate the moment when our current levels of digital excess are no longer feasible. At this point, the prospect of carrying on regardless with growth-driven digital capitalism becomes an even more terrifying option. This would be a future where decent technology access becomes even more skewed toward the elite and the entitled, a future where digital technologies play an even bigger part in our societies becoming more unequal, while continuing to contribute to environmental collapse. All told, this does not come across as a digital future that is worth contemplating, let alone championing.

So, how else might we imagine future forms of digital innovation that are radically different, more aligned with the needs of people, more responsive to the demands of climate-constrained futures and in closer harmony with the needs of nature? This chapter considers some emerging movements that prefigure what these future forms of digital degrowth might look like, and therefore point to necessary shifts in how we conceive the digital. While certainly not the only options open to us, these are all intriguing possibilities for fundamentally reimagining what digital technology can be.

Emerging forms of 'radically sustainable computing'

First, we can turn our attention to several ways in which degrowth principles are beginning to be picked up within computer science, software development and digital activist communities – what was introduced in Chapter 4 as forms of 'radically sustainable computing' (Heikkilä 2021). These provide various examples of how computing can be decoupled from the growth-focused imperatives of capitalist society. Specifically, we can return to complementary areas of emergent thinking such as collapse informatics, computing within limits, permacomputing and digital sufficiency. While still largely conceptual in nature, these propositions are beginning to be developed in various ways, offering alternate visions of how computing hardware might be assembled and powered, alongside radically different approaches to conceptualizing software design and development.

96 Digital Degrowth

Radically sustainable forms of hardware and software

As argued throughout this book, one of the key ambitions of digital degrowth is to move beyond current modes of mass computer hardware production that are unsustainable in terms of their environmental and social impact. The 'salvage computing' movement picks up this theme by looking to extend the use of already available digital hardware and resources and encourage the reuse and recycling of existing computing technology. In its purest form, salvage computing demands an immediate halt to the production of new computing devices and, instead, prioritizes the need to prolong the life of hardware that already exists. Any production of new computing hardware (if deemed necessary) must therefore be based on goals of planned longevity and endurance rather than planned obsolescence.

Salvage computing therefore proposes a completely different approach to hardware, emphasizing the need for rugged design and digital durability. Instead of striving for more environmentally friendly forms of hardware disposal, salvage computing demands that all salvageable elements should be treated as precious resources. Computer designers and manufacturers should seek to maximize the lifespan of all the components used in their products, installing redundancy and bypass mechanisms to keep devices functioning even when various internal components begin to fail, wear out and falter.

These sentiments underpin the emerging idea of 'designing for disassembly', i.e. building computing devices from components that can be reclaimed and reused beyond a device's working life. Sarah Templin (2021) describes this as 'a more concrete, quantifiable approach to ecologically-sound making and consumption'. The practice of reassembling 'new' devices from reclaimed components also gives rise to 'scavenge-friendly' designs for hardware which can be constructed from reclaimed electronic parts and assembled with low-tech tools. Similarly, the 'frugal computing' movement promotes the understanding that computing resources are finite, precious and to be used only when absolutely necessary and in the most efficient ways possible. The underpinning goal of frugal computing is to extend the shelf-life and energy efficiency of successive generations of devices until the point is eventually reached when 'the world will have computing resources that last forever and hardly use any energy' (Vanderbauwhede 2021).

This spirit of durability, resilience and 'doing more with what we already have' is complemented by similar moves in software development. For example, there has been a recent resurgence of minimalist programming approaches as a deliberate push-back against the wasteful 'cut-and-paste' nature of current software development practices enabled by ever-expanding storage capacities and processing speeds. Here, some programming communities are seeking to revive the spirit of computing that flourished in the 1970s and 1980s when limited memory capacity and processing speeds required parsimonious approaches to coding. Such principles are now being revitalized in calls for 'low-level programming' – encouraging software developers and programmers to craft code in ways that seek to decrease processing power – and what Compudanzas (2022) describes as 'writing code closer to the machine'.

Such efforts mark a deliberate move away from the current IT industry tolerance of 'bloatware', where a perpetual 'beta' state of software development encourages programmers to indulge in the continual addition of extraneous code and features. This is seen to result in the lazy and inelegant development of software that inevitably becomes cumbersome and reliant on advanced hardware specifications and processing power to function. As the open-source activist André Staltz (2021) puts it:

> Degrowth in software means that it's okay for your software to be finished and not receive new features. 'Growth' is just a capitalist euphemism for 'bloat'. Nothing in nature grows endlessly, things reach a level of maturity, and they stop there. Same should be true for software.

Putting radically sustainable computing into practice

While these principles and ideals have resulted only in small-scale applications, one-off interventions, speculative designs and similar tentative experiments, movements such as salvage computing and frugal computing certainly offer glimpses of what might be possible. Indeed, a growing number of tangible examples exist of how computing might flourish under such conditions. In terms of digital infrastructure, for example, salvage principles have been used to build and run variations of the local Wi-Fi 'mesh' networks highlighted in Chapter 5, successfully establishing ad hoc forms of networking that do not require corporate datacentres, satellites and cabling. Raghavan and Hassan (2016) outline a salvage internet that can be 'built from scratch' by local communities as and when required. This uses locally salvaged hardware to establish low-tech radio links that are not dependent on high-tech semiconductors and fibre optics. These instances of an 'improvised internet' can span several hundred kilometres and be built and maintained using whatever materials and skills are available locally.

Elsewhere, there are projects such as Collapse O/S – self-contained operating systems that run on 'improvised' computing devices. One application along these lines is the idea of solar-powered websites that can be hosted across networks of solar-powered micro-computers set up to capture sunlight in different locations around the world (De Decker, Otsuka and Abbing 2018; Abbing 2021). Other sustainable design ideas include the notion of 'self-obviating systems' – software and systems that are designed to become steadily more peripheral to the social and cultural systems in which they are embedded. These include speculative designs for social networks which are intended to gradually amass sizable groups of face-to-face contacts and therefore eventually render the online platform of no further benefit to the people who have been using it.

These projects and prototypes are being driven by small groups of sustainability and digital rights activists, technology enthusiasts, academics and community organizers – all looking to form social movements around these alternative forms of digital provision. Each year, various new innovations are celebrated at an annual Computing Within Limits conference that has been running since 2015. Similarly, the Small File Media Festival has run since the beginning of the 2020s to highlight alternative low-carbon approaches to streaming media. Elsewhere, the Green Screen climate justice and digital rights coalition is also working to mobilize low-tech alternate models of what the group terms 'climate-supportive internet infrastructures'. As Fieke Jansen contends: 'the value of these initiatives lies in their ability to challenge the norm of green capitalism and create an alternative infrastructural imaginary' (2023: 62).

Future forms of nature-based computing

Alongside these developments are other emerging areas of computer science that take a completely different line on digital technology and environmental futures – what is sometimes labelled as 'sustainable computing'. These are attempts to look to nature as a means of reimagining computing. The ideas involved diverge radically from conventional IT industry obsessions with optimizing processing power, capability and performance at all costs. Instead, these are visions of 'in the wild' forms of small-scale computing that are enmeshed with ecosystems of water, mud, trees, plants, sunlight and wind. These ideas might sound far-fetched but they are already proving possible. Here, then, are a few other directions that might be pursued long-term to reimagine a future where digital technologies are radically more sustainable and in tune with ecologies and environments.

(i) Nature-powered computing

One innovative area of sustainable computing is energy harvesting, also referred to as energy scavenging and ambient power. This centres around computing devices that collect small amounts of energy from background 'ambient' sources and are not dependent on batteries or other conventional power sources. This is not a new concept. For example, crystal radio sets have been powered by background electromagnetic radiation since the 1910s. Similarly, handheld calculators and watches powered by tiny solar panels proved to be popular consumer products during the 1970s and 1980s. Decades later, these techniques are being revitalized to build computing devices powered by micro-wind turbines or small thermoelectric generators, and even devices that collect energy from stray radio waves. A parallel strand of innovation involves computing devices powered from kinetic energy generated through walking, vibration energy harvesting, and even electrically charged humidity. All these designs are premised on the idea that computing devices used in environments that are already full of naturally occurring energy should not require additional artificially produced energy.

Alongside harnessing ambient energy is the idea of powering computer devices directly from natural materials. Perhaps most advanced in this context are efforts to harness computing energy from soil, wetlands and wastewater. Key here is the use of microbial fuel cells – electrochemical cells that gather minuscule amounts of energy from bacteria (exoelectrogens) living in soil and wastewater. These microbial fuel cells operate at very low voltages, yet researchers have found them sufficient to support the latest forms of low-power computational systems. Interest is therefore growing around the potential of soil-based microbial fuel cells, also known as mud batteries. As Colleen Josephson et al. put it, 'the future of clean computing may be dirty … practical, large-scale, decades-long deployment of soil powered sensing systems is on the horizon' (2022: 14).

One of the main promises around powering low-energy computing devices in these ways is 'untethering' computing from its current reliance on batteries and mains electricity. Again, off-grid and energy independent computing is not a new idea, most notably harking back to developments during the 1990s of hand-crank and wind-up laptops. Crucially, these principles continue to have real-world potential as we approach the middle of the twenty-first century. At the end of the 2010s, Dutch engineers developed a battery-free Nintendo Game Boy as a crude proof-of-concept – powered by a combination of sunlight and kinetic energy generated from the console's buttons (De Winkel et al. 2020). The same team has also developed battery-free Bluetooth devices that run on harvested energy (De Winkel, Tang and Pawełczak 2022).

However, where sustainable computing really gets interesting is when these principles are applied to support radically different computing infrastructures beyond the world of game consoles and other personal devices. Here, researchers imagine sustainable versions of the 'Internet of Things', with millions of small unobtrusive low-power devices embedded across environments, taking sensor measurements, performing calculations and communicating with each other. These devices can be built around ultra-low-power processors that run on harvested energy. Potential applications might include forest-wide networks of sensors that track the movements of wildlife, or ground-based sensors that can provide farmers with information on growing conditions. Alternatively, we might imagine buried and bricked-in sensors that monitor urban infrastructure and buildings, and even medical sensors implanted or ingested into human and non-human bodies.

(ii) Intermittent computing

The idea of background computing that would be capable of looking after itself marks an obvious move away from conventional computer science thinking. It envisages iterations of resilient computing and maintenance-free functioning that move on from current forms of digital technology that are rather more fragile and high-maintenance. The challenge of developing software for devices that are not constantly powered and functioning is being addressed through another key area of sustainable computing innovation – what is termed 'intermittent computing'. Intermittent computing involves the development of devices that slowly harvest and buffer energy when it becomes available, and then operate only when sufficient energy has been banked. Given that ambient sources of energy such as wind, sun and humidity are not constantly available, the software needs to be designed to run until the stored energy is exhausted and a device abruptly powers off, waiting for further energy to be harvested (Lucia et al. 2017).

This mode of computing has clear environmental benefits but also presents some substantial software development challenges. Traditionally, computers are programmed on the assumption that programs will run until they are completed. In contrast, a computer program that is executed intermittently must be capable of spanning power failures – continuously breaking down and restarting hundreds of times each second. This requires new ultra-resilient approaches to programming based on assumptions of inconsistency and imminent breakdown. As Przemyslaw Pawełczak (n.d) puts it: 'To allow near-permanent sensing at low cost and at a reduced ecological impact, we have to rethink how we design these systems. We have to let go of the concept of continuous operation. Batteries must be left behind.'

(iii) Biodegradable computing

Of course, a world full of digital devices running on intermittent ambient energy does little to address the environmental harms arising from the production and disposal of circuit boards, electronic components, silicon chips and so on. In response to this, another important area of sustainable computing innovation is biodegradable computing – organic electronics that are environmentally friendly, low-cost and lightweight (Irimia-Vladu 2014). Again, these are not new ambitions. For example, the development of organic thin-film transistors stretches back to the 1980s, using materials such as are now commonly found in outdoor displays and lighting, solar cells, e-book screens and smart cards. Biodegradable principles are currently being extended into radically different forms of organic computing designed to help us move on from plastics, rare minerals, metals and other environmentally harmful forms of electronics manufacturing. This includes the development of biodegradable printed circuit boards with recoverable and reusable chips (Arroyos et al. 2022), organic electrochemical transistors, and even the world's first wooden transistor – made out of balsa wood by Swedish scientists at the beginning of the 2020s (Van Chinh et al. 2023). Other materials also being experimented with include biodegradable electronics fabricated from paper, synthetic polymers and silk.

All these forms of technology involve manufacturing processes much less complex than is required for conventional circuit boards and transistors. They also use far less energy and resources during their production. However, adopting these materials as the basis for a new generation of computers forces a rethink of some of the fundamental premises of contemporary mass computing – not least computing speed, processing power and consistency. Crucially, these organic semiconductors are substantially slower than conventional electronics, with very low electron mobility in comparison to silicon electronics. Biodegradable computing is also far less uniform in terms of performance. Whereas conventional electronics can be manufactured to function in a regular and consistent manner, the performance of individual components manufactured from organic materials tends to vary considerably from device to device. This means that current IT industry obsessions with efficiency and reliability are not applicable to this form of computing.

As such, it makes little sense to compare these new forms of sustainable computing with the mass-produced forms of digital technology we are currently familiar with. These biodegradable and organic approaches herald a completely different genre of low-power and ambient computing, with devices embedded in natural environments where they can decompose at the end of their lifespans. This implies moving on from a mode of computing where people own multiple personal devices that function solely for their benefit, toward a vision of computing that is rooted in natural environments and works in the background in the interests of the wider ecosystem. This is a world where most computing is not operated or owned by individual consumers and is barely noticeable. As such, it makes little difference that these background forms of computing are powered by wastewater or mud and are slowly rotting away. These are certainly not forms of digital technology that have been over-engineered to appear in sleek, polished and aesthetically attractive forms.

(iv) Fungal computing and other forms of 'wetware'

Perhaps most radical of all are efforts by some sustainable computing researchers to combine low-power computer hardware and software with so-called 'wetware', i.e. chemicals, liquids and even biological living systems. Examples here include exotic-sounding slime-mould computers, plant computers and chemical computers. Efforts have even been made to develop forms of liquid marble computing based on collisions between minuscule droplets of liquid. All these different developments share the aim of harnessing the potential of natural materials to structure and support computational processes.

Perhaps best known of these are the ongoing efforts to harness the electrical activity of mushrooms (more accurately fungal mycelium) to create computing circuits (Adamatzky 2018). Mycelium is the complex web-like root structure of fungi that receives and sends electric signals as the fungus grows, as well as retaining memory of these signals. As such, these roots have the potential to act as electronic components of a computer. Of course, the complex dynamics and system architectures of fungi are wholly different from the circuits and wires of conventional computers. This raises the prospect of completely different networking structures that might allow information to be processed and analysed in new ways, and therefore support novel forms of computing and sensing. In reality, any form of fungal computing will operate at much slower rates than today's machines. Yet, while lacking in conventional expectations of speed, this form of computing has numerous other advantages – not least the ability to grow naturally and expand, to self-repair and self-regenerate, and to run on only very small amounts of energy.

104 Digital Degrowth

Again, cutting-edge developments such as these raise radically different possibilities for what computing might be. Fungal computing is not intended as a direct replacement for digital computing as we currently know it. Indeed, some computer scientists are researching how these fungal logics of processing information might be used to augment current digital information systems. Other groups of researchers are working to develop fungi computing as a complementary form of environmental sensing. Here, it is envisaged that connecting to fungal networks might allow large flows of data to be monitored over wide geographic areas. This could be used to monitor what is going on in an ecosystem, using natural materials such as mycelium as large-scale underground environmental sensors (Dehshibi and Adamatzky 2021).

Anticipating a new wave of nature-based computing

At first glance, these nature-based computing innovations seem utterly alien in comparison to the forms of personal computing and digital devices that have dominated over the past few decades. Indeed, one of the leading sustainable computing R&D centres goes under the banner of 'The Unconventional Computing Lab'. Working to develop fungal networks and mud batteries might appear unconventional to many lay people, but it is perhaps no less far-fetched than the concept of cloud-based computing would have seemed when explained in the 1980s. Indeed, being open to the prospect of new forms of computing built around natural resources such as mud, wastewater, balsa wood and fungi should not be too difficult a stretch. After all, our smartphones, laptops and servers are currently dependent on battery packs that are packed full of graphite, lithium salts, metal oxides and other fast-depleting materials. So, why should we not consider using more plentiful natural resources such as wastewater and mud? Similarly, the idea of natural materials playing a key role in digital infrastructures is already a reality. Given that current computing is dependent on networks constructed from copper, why not be open to the idea of networks made of other materials, particularly if they are naturally occurring and self-sustaining?

These proposals offer a vision of computing that is not massively environmentally harmful in terms of resource extraction,

Future Innovations

toxic e-waste and other harms associated with current forms of digital technology manufacture, use and disposal. Indeed, they raise the possibility of radically different scales of computing that are in step with future environmental needs. For example, sustainable computing encourages us to imagine forms of computing that are entwined with nature and integrated into our natural environments, and do not drain and deplete finite resources. These forms computing are deliberately slowed down and sporadic, rather than being accelerated and always-on, and are designed to decay back into the earth and literally become part of the environment.

Yet, these technologies also offer a completely new vision of how and why computing might be deployed. Crucially, such forms of computing exist primarily to help care for natural ecosystems and environments. For example, in a world of water shortages and drought, it makes good sense to have soil moisture-sensing systems that advise farmers when and where to water crops. In a world where essential man-made infrastructures face constant risks from extreme weather and natural disasters it seems prudent to have low-powered underground monitoring systems in situ. In a world where we need to preserve as much of the planet's natural habitat as possible, it seems obvious to develop sensing systems that can support biodiversity and conservation – systems that can anticipate everything from the start of wildfires to the safe movement of wildlife. These are all forms of computing that can work for the good of our ecosystems rather than to their detriment. In times of climate collapse and ecological instability, why would we *not* want to take this next generation of sustainable digital innovation seriously?

Conclusions

All these examples – and the broader principles that underpin them – offer rich provocations to think otherwise about digital technology in an era of scarce resourcing and climate breakdown. Ideas of salvage computing, minimal programming and wetware networks challenge everyone concerned with issues of technology and sustainability to imagine alternative forms of computing that can be put to radically different ends. As Bill Tomlinson (n.d) puts it, such movements seek 'to bring about new kinds of computing systems that might allow us as a civilization to more effectively engage with these sets of [environmental] issues'. Indeed, one of the key themes running through the examples in this chapter is the need to radically rethink how digital technology is both composed from, but also impacts on, natural environments and ecosystems. All the examples therefore push us into contemplating what engaging with digital technology along material and planetary lines might mean in practical terms. They are unfamiliar and uncomfortable proposals, presenting digital technologies that we are usually conditioned to think of as cleanly designed and neatly packaged in decidedly dirty, organic and untamed ways. They might appear to be wildly ambitious and experimental, but they give some sense of how digital technology can be reimagined along radically different lines: 'As our species currently faces an unprecedented existential threat, it is time for such bold experimentations to be brought to the fore and inspire much-needed steps towards genuine change' (Kostakis, Niaros and Giotitsas 2023: 2320).

While they might feel raw and unsettling, examples such as mud batteries and mycelium computing foreground the environmental and ecological entanglements of digital technology. They highlight the need for future forms of digital degrowth to recognize that 'nature has its own interests' (Washington et al. 2018) and that digital technologies are only viable in the long term if they are genuinely aligned with the planet's ecosystems and ecologies. These are scaled-back forms of digital technology that embody the idea that human life needs to be better aligned with the maintenance and regeneration of environmental and ecological cycles. It therefore makes sense for future forms of digital innovation to engage with natural environments as sources of support and innovation, and generally exist in ways that are in harmony – rather than conflict – with the natural world.

In short, the examples outlined in this chapter suggest how digital technology can be reimagined as a balanced partnership between people and nature. They highlight the long-term need to move beyond the goal of simply reducing costs and the harms that digital technologies impose on the natural environment, i.e. to simply have technology that is 'environmentally friendly' or 'environmentally aware'. These examples push us to contemplate new forms of digital innovation that are intrinsically bound up with – and perhaps even led by – natural resources and environments. These are long-term ambitions, yet this chapter offers a sense of what such new forms of digital innovation might look like. The key question to now consider is what would be required for us to reach such a state of digital reinvention and revitalization. This provides the impetus for the final chapter. What will it take to put any of the ideas outlined over the past two chapters into action? How can we set about enacting these different strands of digital degrowth?

7

Where Now?
Everywhere But Here!

Introduction

This book has built a case for rethinking our relationships with digital technology in ways that do not simply perpetuate the core problems and fault lines of the current digital malaise. At the moment, mainstream calls for 'Green Tech' and 'Tech for Good' are not concerned with forcing a substantial break from the current status quo. Indeed, the best that Green Tech plans from the likes of Google and Microsoft can offer is a carbon-neutral continuation of digital capitalism. In contrast, degrowth thinking raises possibilities for change that are not often foregrounded in mainstream discussions of digital society. Degrowth thinking challenges us to imagine what the world might look like if we were to decouple digital technology from the imperatives of economic growth and instead refashion our collective understandings of the digital through the values and politics of social justice and environmental sustainability.

Reimagining digital technology through degrowth principles and ideals might seem unduly challenging, but it is a wholly appropriate response to the fast-changing nature of planetary and societal conditions. We have moved well past the point where the IT industry and its financiers should be given free rein do whatever they like in the name of innovation and boundary-pushing. Instead, digital degrowth calls for communitarian forms of digital development that can lay the foundations for more democratic and restrained forms of living. These are changes that need to be enacted at many different levels, starting with local practices but also stimulating radical global imaginaries. They need to be driven by local social movements, coalescing into a broader commons situated well outside the influence of transnational corporations and venture capitalists. Now that we have reached the final chapter of this book, the key challenge is to work out ways of practically realizing these broad ambitions.

Building a vision of digital degrowth

The various discussion points and ongoing conversations that have been developed over the past six chapters will need to continue for some time to come. One key point of action will be sustaining dialogue around the possibilities of digital degrowth. Indeed, any degrowth transition will require a strong initial push to force 'narrative shifts' (Jansen et al. 2023) and engage people in a period of 'vision building' (Frenzel et al. 2023). This will mean persuasively debunking popular received wisdoms that industry-led Green Growth solutions will somehow come good and permit the continued unproblematic development of digital capitalism. The idea of digital degrowth calls such complacency into question. As we saw in Chapter 2, it seems highly unlikely that genuinely sustainable digital conditions will result from the continued economic power of a few Big Tech corporations, private ownership of digital infrastructure, and the underpinning imperative to attract investment. Instead of holding out for neat technical fixes that would allow for continued digital growth (albeit with a green veneer), concerted efforts are needed to reframe common understandings around 'tak[ing] the notion of *limits* seriously' (Sætra 2023).

Another aspect of digital degrowth is the idea of looking back to past forms of computing and digital innovation to reclaim practices, processes and ideas that have been left behind in the rush for continual progress. The past few chapters have shown that there is value in rediscovering low-tech approaches such as single-board computers and shared devices. Yet it is important to stress that this is not simply a sentimental longing to return to past forms of 'retro' computing. Many of the original incarnations of open-source computing and hobbyist IT communities were highly problematic in terms of their sexism, racism, classism and other exclusionary politics. Digital degrowth is not simply a call for an unmediated return to past forms of computing, but rather a challenge to pick out and revitalize past computing practices that can enhance human well-being today. It is a question of reimagining past ways of computing in retooled forms that are fit for the challenges that will increasingly define the remainder of the twenty-first century.

Further work is also needed to publicize the highly progressive and innovative nature of the digital degrowth position. The ideas advanced in this book chime with Pansera and Fressoli's (2021) notion of 'post-growth forms of innovation' that are led through bottom-up initiatives and stewarded by grassroots organizations, social cooperatives and other forms of open and collaborative production. In this sense, digital degrowth is not anti-innovation, but a bold attempt to move innovation away from corporations, markets, governments, military funding and ambitions of stimulating and accelerating economic growth (Strand et al. 2018). If we are seeking a long-term transition away from the current hegemony of digital excess, then taking a degrowth stance toward digital technology offers a realistic platform from which to innovate for real change.

Finally, it is important to connect the digital-specific concerns laid out across this book with wider pushes for other broader transitions to degrowth. Any call for digital degrowth needs to be in clear solidarity with hundreds of other degrowth efforts in areas ranging from agriculture to energy and employment. As such, the ideas and agendas in this book need to be seen as part of a much wider 'cohesive degrowth agenda' (Liegey and Nelson 2020: 116). Any use of digital technologies must be part of a wider transition that establishes an acceptable balance between human development and the utilization of natural resources. On the one hand, this means putting digital technology into correspondence with social movements pushing for deliberative democracy, self-provisioning, the 'right to repair' and resource sharing in other areas of everyday life. On the other hand, it means promoting forms of digital technology that might support wider degrowth ambitions around the equitable downsizing of economic growth and consumption. To reiterate, digital degrowth does not simply mean pushing for *less* use of digital technology. Rather, it pushes us to develop ways of using digital technology that are genuinely of collective benefit, that work outside of economic growth imperatives, and that are clearly not causing environmental harm. Any form of digital innovation that helps us to fulfil these ambitions is welcome.

What might digital degrowth look like in practice?

Digital degrowth implies a fundamental shift in how we collectively make sense of the digital future; its concern is with how much digital technology is necessary and beneficial (in societal and planetary terms), as opposed to how much digital technology is possible and/or profitable. At this point, it is important to reiterate that there is no single agreed-upon way in which digital degrowth 'must be done'. This is something that local communities and societies need to collectively work out for themselves. Degrowth prioritizes consensual and democratic approaches to experimenting, negotiating and deciding on what forms of digital technology might be appropriate for local communities and contexts. This implies regularly re-evaluating on a collective basis what might be needed and/or be desirable, and conversely what limits need to be applied.

These are unfamiliar ways of thinking about digital technology, yet it is certainly possible to begin to imagine what digital degrowth might look like in practice. Take, for example, what it might mean for future forms of what is currently framed as 'personal' computing. Although the days of digital excess will have long passed, this would not be a world completely devoid of digital technology. Your local community might have decided that every household should have access to a laptop as a basic requisite for ensuring 'good lives for all' (Hickel and Sullivan 2024). In this case, households might have access to a robust modular laptop (which everyone in the house can use when necessary) on long-term loan from their local device sharing hub. The idea of a 'device for life' is encouraged, with communal hardware maintained and kept working through local repair hubs.

While there might not be any official restrictions, these devices would mostly be used occasionally – brought out for low-bandwidth activities that people find enriching and worthwhile.

112   Digital Degrowth

While some people would have little need to ever use a device, others might want to post on community forums with offers of skill swaps or local volunteer work, keep in touch with distant relatives, or occasionally download open-access media to be consumed offline. Big resource-hungry forms of computing would be prioritized for matters of national importance, or for uses of massive computing power that are considered 'essential to the common good' (Pitron 2023: 223). For example, there may well be good reasons for medical researchers and climate scientists to be using powerful AI. But the use of this sort of computing (and the few sustainable data centres in the world needed to power it) would be strictly restricted to 'public good' missions. This is a world where only a limited amount of digital technology use takes place, as and when it is genuinely useful and enriching.

Of course, this sort of digital lifestyle might appear unthinkable when set against our current mode of 'always-on' digital dependency. Yet, it is worth remembering that any digital downsizing would not take place in isolation. Digital degrowth will occur alongside many other degrowth transitions, in a world where we will have also become accustomed to radical changes in how often we drive cars, take flights or go shopping. People who are leading scaled-back and more satisfying lives in general would not feel particularly inconvenienced by being unable to continuously access a device. Indeed, a degrowth transition seeks to enable people to collectively rethink the values, purposes and forms of how they live and work, as well as the values, purposes and forms of the technologies that can help them do this.

This shift in perspective can be illustrated by anticipating what digital degrowth might look like for a local school. Education is an interesting context to view through a digital degrowth lens – not least because schools in many countries are currently infused by digital devices, platforms, software and systems. This means that there is plenty of irredeemable digital technology use that a local school community might collectively decide to put a stop to. Why should all students be required to 'Bring Your Own Device'? Why do books, tests and quizzes need to be online? Why should schools be running sophisticated digital surveillance software? These are all digital excesses that a school community might understandably decide to immediately withdraw from, developing a collective confidence to rediscover analogue practices and offline processes that fulfil the same purposes. Conversely, a school community might also decide to invest its energies in technology practices that it considers more convivial in nature. A forward-thinking school might choose to run a repair café, device sharing library or similar venture that draws on the expertise and skills of students, parents, grandparents, teachers and others living nearby.

In the longer term, there are the more existential challenges of deciding what forms of education provision a local community might want to support. In this context, it could be argued that some of the most 'manipulative tools' of contemporary society are education institutions such as mass schooling – which Ivan Illich described as discouraging people 'from taking control of their own learning' and engaging with other educational opportunities within their immediate communities (1971: 8). Seen along these lines, then, digital technologies might instead be used to support alternative forms of community learning that are genuinely accessible and beneficial to all. School teachers might choose to participate in 'knowledge exchanges' and 'tuition exchanges' – platforms allowing people to offer tutoring in their own areas of expertise in return for being tutored in other areas that they wish to become more knowledgeable in. Digital degrowth might push local communities toward developing new forms of 'open education' platforms that support 'the creation of networks, as opposed to institutions, that are temporary, autonomous, and non-hierarchical, and facilitate a variety of diverse models of learning and community interaction' (Todd 2012: 78). In short, digital degrowth does not simply mean taking technology out of schools. Rather, it is an opportunity to rethink altogether what sorts of education we want to encourage, and what forms of digital technology might support this.

Moving toward digital degrowth – ongoing challenges

As these brief examples imply, working through the practicalities of how such transitions to digital degrowth might be initiated will be a major undertaking. Here, then, are a few of the challenges that will need to be addressed.

114 Digital Degrowth

(i) Digital degrowth as a matter of social transformation

The idea of digital degrowth certainly constitutes a major social transformation – challenging the status quo of digital capitalism and changing the fundamental conditions of how we live with digital technologies. This is not simply a matter of persuading individuals to change their digital practices, or working to influence people's attitudes, behaviours and choices. Indeed, as we saw in Chapter 1, the current mode of digital excess did not come about purely through individual choices and consumer preferences. Instead, large-scale transition to digital degrowth involves the huge challenge of changing social practices around digital technology. This entails nothing less than establishing a new regime of what digital technology is in terms of infrastructure and tools, modes of access and governance, forms of know-how, social conventions and routines – all of which needs to take hold across all aspects of everyday life and society.

Here, then, it is helpful to think about a transition to digital degrowth in terms of the different elements that make up social practice – what Elizabeth Shove (2023) identifies as materials, competences and meanings. The previous two chapters have given plenty of examples of what digital degrowth might look like in terms of devices, components, physical infrastructure and the materials they might be made from. At the same time, we have also begun to sketch out how digital degrowth relates to various different ways of 'doing' technology (skills, know-how, techniques), as well as a distinct set of ideas, aspirations and visions for how and why digital technologies might play a role in degrowth society. The big challenge now is to work out how connections can begin to be made *between* these different elements of digital degrowth, and lasting social change be put into motion.

So, what might this look like in practice? One key aspect of any social transformation is unmaking the hegemonic conditions that precede it. In this sense, this book has outlined various ways in which groups and movements might work to hinder, challenge and break up the dominant conditions of digital excess, and create conditions where once-normal practices begin to disappear and be seen as undesirable and/or downright unacceptable. In turn, these efforts will need to be accompanied by the promotion of diversified alternative ways of 'doing' digital technology that people can encounter on a regular basis – what Shove, Pantzar

Where Now? Everywhere But Here! 115

and Watson describe as 'initial moments when "proto-practices" emerge and become real' (2012: 15). Crucial here, however, is the need for such practices to become sustained across different moments and places. This will involve working to support digital degrowth practices in societal domains that connect the everyday lives of large numbers of people – such as education, health and urban planning. Efforts such as these can create connections and convergences between different digital degrowth practices, encouraging 'bundles' of practices to emerge across people's everyday lives and the wider society.

All told, there will be much work to do to stimulate and sustain the significant social change that digital degrowth implies. This will involve rebuilding the material and moral infrastructure of our societies in ways that are scaled-back, slowed-down and communally oriented – to the point that our current modes of digital excess and digital dependency simply make no sense. It will require working out ways to move away from conditions where a smartphone is deemed necessary to access welfare payments or other public services. It will also require encouraging cooperative (rather than competitive) cultures where social status is not derived from owning the latest model of smartwatch, where engaging in environmentally harmful uses of digital technology is commonly understood to be unacceptable, and where offline and non-digital alternatives are promoted and prioritized. In short, we need to establish conditions where digital degrowth practices are seen as commonsense and experienced as practically fulfilling and intrinsically rewarding. Establishing such social arrangements will not be easy but is certainly possible.

(ii) The limits of local determinism

Any practical transition to degrowth will involve the introduction of localized, cooperative modes of production, consumption and maintenance that begin to challenge existing forms of large-scale manipulative digital technology. Most of the changes imagined over the past few chapters are most likely to start as 'bottom-up' actions and shifts grounded in the efforts of local groups and communities to alter their own practices. The success of digital degrowth will therefore depend on the strength and reach of local groups and communities in initiating this work of reimagining and stewarding digital provision and processes.

116   Digital Degrowth

Again, this will not be an easy transition and it suggests that digital degrowth is most likely to take hold in localities where social cohesiveness, cooperation and solidarity are already strong. However, it is important not to over-romanticize what a future of self-determinism and collective organization might look like (Wainwright and Mann 2018). Indeed, degrowth thinking can justifiably be criticized for idealizing notions of 'community' and 'local' while underplaying the exclusionary and oppressive dynamics that can often pervade community-based and cooperative efforts. Community-building will undoubtedly be one of the hardest ongoing aspects of digital degrowth. As Giorgos Kallis et al. acknowledge, 'communal projects must negotiate inclusion and exclusion, horizontal and vertical relations, as they address tensions and contradictions in the consolidation of common values and meanings' (2020: 61).

What form these local actions might take now needs to be the focus for further elaboration. First, local communities need to be engaged in matters of technology governance, in particular the prioritization of local sovereignty in determining what is done with digital technology. Here, digital degrowth challenges us to develop new forms of localized governance imbued with place-based, context-specific approaches to digital resource management, planning and enactment. There are various ways this might be achieved. For example, it might be led by grassroots collectives that incorporate community voices in determining democratic, fairer and workable deployments of technology within local settings. The hope here is that working outside state and IT industry imperatives will lead to the articulation of very different agendas and approaches.

Second, there are issues of scale. The emphasis on 'bottom-up' grassroots approaches implies a practical politics of digital technology that reframes people's efforts along the lines of social movements. Key here is the idea of alliances being formed within local spaces and local collectives, for example between local libraries, schools, neighbourhood IT professionals, repair cafés and other interested parties. These efforts can generate participatory, deliberative and non-hierarchical relations between residents, interest groups and institutions, and ensure the co-development of locally appropriate actions. If successful, these small-scale local experiments can be aggregated and extended to other settings, drawing on 'concerted social movement action across geographical scales that can make these possibilities (and large-scale state transformation) possible' (Routledge, Cumbers and Derickson 2018: 85).

One key question is the extent to which local groups can use digital technologies to link up and network with like-minded others. Such networks can be established between local groups in many ways. For some, digital telecommunications might well have an important role to play in connecting local degrowth groups together on a larger scale, allowing the exchange of expertise, online resources, information and inspiration through a process of what Vasilis Kostakis terms 'cosmolocalism'. Of course, this does not require retaining the digital networks that we currently have, or indeed the continuation of global digital networks at all. While digital technologies might be a useful means of bringing some local degrowth efforts together, international solidarity is not (and has never been) fully dependent on digital networks. There are also many offline ways for local communities to interact, share and collaborate with others 'in ways that prioritise local autonomy and cultural diversity but also a sense of global common benefit' (Kostakis, Niaros and Giotitsas 2023: 2311).

(iii) Dealing with vested interests

Clearly, any attempt to disrupt the highly profitable machinations of the digital economy will face sustained hostility and opposition from vested corporate and financial interests. Any such effort will also face hostility and opposition from mainstream technologists and technology communities who feel threatened by the idea of technological progress and digital innovation being somehow restrained. As Kōhei Saitō suggests, one of the major dilemmas that now faces any transition toward degrowth is working out ways to 'overcome ... domination by huge corporations like Google, Apple, Facebook, Amazon in order to wrest our powers of imagination back and find a new path towards a new future' (2024: 147).

Any effort to support the transition to digital degrowth will therefore need to be mindful of the economic interests and political power of the industries and professions that it is seeking to usurp. This will clearly be a long-running – but not insurmountable – challenge. As a start, IT companies already interested in social justice and environmental sustainability can be pushed to introduce explicit degrowth dimensions into their product designs and business models. For example, Chapter 5 began to imagine how change might be forced from within IT firms and Big Tech corporations. The idea of reinventing and revitalizing digital society can be pitched in ways that resonate with tech workers who pride themselves on being problem-driven. Digital degrowth certainly constitutes a genuinely complicated and worthwhile problem for the tech industry's brightest minds to devote their time to – in stark contrast to devoting their careers to working out ways to more effectively target online advertising and clickbait content.

These ambitions to change corporate culture are not unachievable. Such changes might start by making modest demands on the tech industry's time and resources – as a side-hustle for interested workers or as part of a company's volunteering and 'corporate social responsibility' obligations. After low-stakes activities such as these are in place, more substantive actions can be introduced. While we should not underestimate the power of multinational corporations to protect their profits, we should also not discount the motivations of the thousands of professionals and experts that these corporations are ultimately dependent on. There are many IT workers who undoubtedly feel ambivalent about the societal consequences of their work, and who worry that their professional lives and careers are perhaps lacking in moral substance. Digital degrowth offers a worthwhile alternative vision of how these professionals might choose to make use of their expertise and wisdom.

(iv) Forcing governments and states into action

The relationship between degrowth ambitions and governments is not straightforward. At present, nearly every government has vested interests in sustaining economic growth. While support for degrowth as a sustainability strategy is increasing amongst academics, environmentalists and progressive-minded economists, fears remain that it is still too radical for mainstream politicians to accept. As stressed throughout this book, it is important to remember that any transition toward digital degrowth will be driven initially through bottom-up actions, and wider take up driven through ongoing struggles, conflict and resistance. As Meredith Whittaker (2023) observes, tech critics often make the mistake of imagining a supreme benevolent state authority that is willing to 'do what's right' when it comes to public interest

Where Now? Everywhere But Here!

technology – bravely regulating Big Tech companies and holding them accountable for their environmental harms. Yet, all the harmful aspects of digital capitalism that degrowth seeks to redress have come about with the support (at least tacitly) of governments and states. Most governments and states will need to be cajoled, coerced and compelled into taking up the mantle of digital degrowth.

So, while governments should not be relied upon to initiate transitions to digital degrowth, more thought needs to be given to how they can be used to broaden initial efforts. If, as Kallis, Mastini and Zografos (2023) suggest, there is a growing appetite for radical sustainability opinions amongst some elected policymakers, then the idea of finding official support for digital degrowth might be feasible. In this spirit, where cracks can be found within policy thinking, it is certainly worth seeding ideas that are aligned with the spirit of digital degrowth. These might include 'push' measures that target IT industry production, alongside 'pull' measures that focus on changing the consumption patterns of the wealthier technology users. This might also include reversing any government policy that encourages excessive digitization – such as tax breaks, regulation exemptions and other incentives designed to attract Big Tech corporations.

Governments might also be encouraged to support the kinds of degrowth-friendly technologies outlined in previous chapters (such as public provisioning of devices and right to repair), and to introduce bans on IT industry advertising and other egregious business practices. Governments and states can also be pushed for a 'digital divestment' on the part of their services and agencies, i.e. instigating alternatives to the digital systems and infrastructures currently used to mediate people's everyday engagements with social welfare, healthcare and education services. While governments will not lead us toward a state of digital degrowth on their own, they can still be a useful part of our efforts.

Moving toward digital degrowth – next steps

Transition to a state of digital degrowth will clearly be difficult but is by no means unachievable. There is now growing popular support for rethinking the roles that digital technology plays in our societies, and a burgeoning sense that a hard reset is required.

120 Digital Degrowth

Moving forward, however, raises some tough questions. For example, who are the most willing advocates and protagonists of any digital degrowth moment? How might the idea of digital degrowth become more widely understood and ultimately politically impactful? How can degrowth approaches to digital technology be best 'framed and governed in emergent regional powers like China, Russia, India or emerging economies in Africa and Latin America' (Pansera, Ehlers and Kerschner 2019)? What role can different groups play in developing digital degrowth as politics?

In the first instance, some strong starting points already exist from which to begin building digital degrowth as a social movement – not least the wider momentum of ongoing public push-backs and community organization against climate collapse, Black Lives Matter, and other social movements coalescing around progressive socio-environmental change. The digital degrowth movement has clear synergies and points of connection with these allied movements. At the same time, digital degrowth needs to be established within tech circles as a grassroots, community-led movement that fosters solidarity between software developers and community organizers, local repair cultures and hacker groups, digital rights activists, those who are currently technologically privileged, and those currently disadvantaged groups that stand to benefit most from future uses of digital technology. If such alliances can be established and sustained, then there are good grounds to hope that digital degrowth ideas can be advanced through collective efforts that bring together technical expertise, communitarian ideals and post-capitalist politics.

Key here is seeing digital degrowth as part of a broader transition to a degrowth society. Degrowth, post-growth and similar agendas are gaining momentum around the world, and in one sense this book is simply arguing for digital technology to be brought more fully into these wider efforts. At the same time, digital degrowth advocates need to reach out to engage others who do not see themselves as post-capitalists but are nevertheless thinking along similar lines. There are many different constituencies who are beginning to push back against the environmental costs of the artificial intelligence and data industries, who are disenchanted with rampant online consumerism, digital inequalities, digital overwork and similar. A strong desire for rethinking our relationships with digital technology is already being articulated (if implicitly) through the growing public concern and consumer dissatisfaction of tech users in the Global North. One initial task for the nascent digital degrowth movement is to begin publicizing such commonalities – bringing people together around these shared concerns and collectively finding ways to work together to achieve change.

Exactly where such efforts progress will need to be a matter of collective discussion and deliberation. Indeed, the ideas sketched out in this book are an invitation for ongoing dialogue. Digital degrowth is not an idealistic predefined roadmap for the immediate wholesale rejection of current digital conditions and the establishment of global collective action. Instead, digital degrowth is an invitation to begin thinking more imaginatively about what else digital technology might be. This book has brought together a grab-bag of ideas that need to be further discussed, dissected and developed. Any actions will need to be entered into as experiments and provocations – some of them will fail quickly, but others might offer glimpses of viable alternatives. The key aim of beginning to think and act along such lines is to unsettle the current hegemony of excessive digital production, consumption and disposal, and to show that alternative forms of 'digital society' are possible. As Giorgos Kallis and colleagues put it, 'the goal [of degrowth] is not to replace one monoculture with another. It is to create conditions that support the development of more vibrant realms of possibility with different rhythms, purposes and scales.' (2020: 58)

While this might sound straightforward, we need to acknowledge the profoundly unsettling nature of the general idea of degrowth transitions. Indeed, while ideas such as digital repair cafés and single-board computers might come across as somewhat mundane, ultimately digital degrowth is an ontological challenge to rethink the future in terms that can admittedly feel beyond our full comprehension. It is an invitation to give sustained thought to existential threats such as climate collapse and societal breakdown that can feel too big to contemplate, let alone address. Anticipating different forms of digital technology for an age of climate crisis and societal instability is not simply a case of taking stock of digital capitalism's failings and coming up with a neat Plan B. Instead, it is a drawn-out process of working out how to make sense of something that is fundamentally

122   Digital Degrowth

unknowable, far bigger than us, and that threatens our entire sense of well-being.

As such, the idea of digital degrowth raises the uncomfortable (and perhaps unwelcome) challenge that everything we have so far become accustomed to during our lifetimes is no longer fit for the world that we will soon be living in. Taken at face value, concerns around the environmental burdens of data centres in Mexico or the practicalities of salvage computing seem too intangible to take seriously, let alone act upon. Yet, embracing these shifts in perspective is necessary if we are to work out a plausible digital future for an impending era when things are going to be very different. Developing these new understandings will inevitably be process of ongoing reconciliation that we are all going to have to work toward for years to come. Digital technology is just a small part of the adjustments that will have to be made, but it is as good a place as anywhere to start grappling with such existential challenges.

Conclusions

These are not ideas, arguments and agendas that any reader will *fully* agree with. In one sense, this book is a provocation – an attempt to see how far these arguments can be taken. Exactly what each reader takes from the book is less important that the fact that they take something from it. Some people might already be fully on board with the idea of degrowth transitions, and hopefully this book will prompt further thought on the role that digital technologies might have in a degrowth society. Others might remain unconvinced by the prospect of a post-capitalist society, but still recognize the need to rethink the material and ethical bases of digital technology and/or the idea of seeing digital technology within limits. Hopefully this book offers insight into what might be needed to strive for genuinely new and impactful forms of digital sustainability. Some might simply remain uneasy about the harmful directions in which digital capitalism appears to be heading; hopefully this book provides some starting points for continuing to think about how we might work toward better forms of digital technology, and what we might consider 'better' to mean.

Regardless of our own current priorities and personal politics, we can hopefully agree that the forms of digital technology production, consumption and disposal that have come to define our societies over the past few decades are not working and are unsustainable. This book has presented some suggestions for how things might be otherwise – the first step toward which is collectively agreeing that change and transition away from excessive growth-driven digitization *is* possible. Beyond this, the idea of digital degrowth raises a range of possibilities. It is now up to all of us to collectively work out what changes and transitions we want to see, and how these might be achieved. There is plenty of reason to believe that better digital futures are possible . . . we need to all pursue this belief as courageously as possible.

References

Abbing, R. (2021). This is a solar-powered website, which means it sometimes goes offline. *LIMITS '21: Workshop on Computing within Limits*, June.

Adamatzky, A. (2018). Towards fungal computer. *Interface Focus* 8(6): 20180029.

Ahern, A. (2023a). Red and green make ... degrowth. *Los Angeles Review of Books*, 23 July.

Ahern, A. (2023b). Twitter, 29 December, https://twitter.com/PoliticOf Nature/status/1740562195048714713.

Ahmed, A. (2024). Hammering it out. *XRDS: Crossroads* 30(4): 46–9.

Alexander, S. (2015). Simplicity. In D'Alisa, G., Demaria, F. and Kallis, G. (eds). *Degrowth: A Vocabulary for a New Era*. Routledge.

Ames, M. (2019). *The Charisma Machine*. MIT Press.

Andreessen, M. (2023). Techno-Optimist Manifesto, https://a16z.com /the-techno-optimist-manifesto.

Arroyos, V., Viitaniemi, M., Keehn, N., Oruganti, V., Saunders, W., Strauss, K., Iyer, V. and Nguyen, B. (2022). A tale of two mice. *CHI Conference on Human Factors in Computing Systems Extended Abstracts*, pp. 1–10.

Aula, V. and Bowles, J. (2023). Stepping back from data and AI for good. *Big Data & Society* 10(1): 20539517231173901.

Bacevic, J. (2021). Unthinking knowledge production. *Globalizations* 18(7): 1206–18.

Barbas Babtista, G. (2020). Free software. In Treu, N., Schmelzer, M. and Burkhart, C. (eds). *Degrowth in Movement(s)*. Zero Books.

References

BBC News (2024). Data centre power use 'to surge six-fold in 10 years', 28 March, bbc.com.

Becker, C. (2023). *Insolvent: How to Reorient Computing for Just Sustainability*. MIT Press.

Benjamin, R. (2019). *Race Against Technology*. Polity.

Bennett, J. (1987). Review: the whale and the reactor. *Political Theory* 15(4): 662–4.

Berners-Lee, T. (2010). Long live the web. *Scientific American*, 1 December.

Bhowmik, S. (2019). The battery is the message. *Communication+1* 7(2): 1–27.

Birch, K. and Bronson, K. (2022). Big tech. *Science as Culture* 31(1): 1–14.

Boston Consulting Group (2023). How AI can speed climate action. November, bcg.com.

Boulding, K. (1966). The economics of the coming Spaceship Earth. In H. Jarrett (ed). *Environmental Quality in a Growing Economy*. Johns Hopkins University Press, pp. 3–14.

Bradley, K. (2018). Bike kitchens: spaces for convivial tools. *Journal of Cleaner Production* 197: 1676–83.

Brain, T. and Lavigne, S. (2024). All that is air melts into air. *e-flux*, June, e-flux.com.

Brock, A. (2020). *Distributed Blackness*. New York University Press.

Brueckner M. (2013). Corporation as psychopath. In Idowu, S., Capaldi, N., Zu, L. and Gupta, A. (eds). *Encyclopedia of Corporate Social Responsibility*. Springer, pp. 613–18.

Campolo, A. and Crawford, K. (2020). Enchanted determinism. *Engaging Science, Technology and Society* 6: 1–19.

Carter, J. and Yang, M. (2023). Sophie vs. the Machine: neo-luddism as response to technical-colonial corruption of the general intellect. *Rhetoric Society Quarterly* 53(3): 366–78.

Casilli, A. (2024). *Waiting for Robots*. University of Chicago Press.

Christophers, B. (2024). *The Price is Wrong*. Verso.

Ciacci, J. (2023). 'We are struggling to survive': resistance against mining in Acacoyagua, Chiapas. In Tierra Común Network (eds). *Resisting Data Colonialism*. Institute of Network Cultures, Amsterdam, pp. 51–6.

Compudanzas (2022). Low-level programming. February, compudanzas.net.

Constine, J. (2017). Mark Zuckerberg's humanitarian manifesto. *TechCrunch*, 16 February.

Costanza-Chock, S. (2020). *Design Justice*. MIT Press.

Cox, P. (2023). Vélomobility is to degrowth as automobility is to growth. *Applied Mobilities* 8(3): 265–85.

References

Crampton, J. (2024). How digital geographies render value: geofences, the blockchain, and the possibilities of slow alternatives. In Glückler, J. and Panitz, R. (eds). *Knowledge and Digital Technology*. Springer, pp. 257–79.

Crary, J. (2022). *Scorched Earth*. Verso.

Crawford, K. (2024). Generative AI's environmental costs are soaring – and mostly secret. *Nature*, 20 February.

Crawford, K. and Joler, V. (2018). *Anatomy of an AI system*. AI Now Institute & Share Lab, 7 September, anatomyof.ai.

Daly, H. (1972). In defence of a steady state. *American Journal of Agricultural Economics* 54(5): 945–54.

Davies, W. (2022). Destination unknown. *London Review of Books*, 9 June.

De Decker, K., Otsuka, M. and Abbing, R. (2018). How to build a low-tech website? *Low←Tech Magazine*, 24 September, solar.lowtech magazine.com.

De Winkel, J., Kortbeek, V., Hester, J. and Pawełczak, P. (2020). Battery-free game boy. *Proceedings of the ACM on Interactive, Mobile, Wearable and Ubiquitous Technologies* 4(3): 1–34.

De Winkel, J., Tang, H. and Pawełczak, P. (2022). Intermittently powered Bluetooth that works. In *MobiSys 2022: Proceedings of the 2022 20th Annual International Conference on Mobile Systems, Applications and Services*. Association for Computing Machinery, pp. 287–301.

Dehshibi, M. and Adamatzky, A. (2021). Electrical activity of fungi. *Biosystems*, https://doi.org/10.1016/j.biosystems.2021.104373.

Deriu, M. (2015). Conviviality. In D'Alisa, G., Demaria, F. and Kallis. G. (eds). *Degrowth: A Vocabulary for a New Era*. Routledge.

Doctorow, C. (2024). 'Enshittification' is coming for absolutely everything. *Financial Times*, 8 February.

Dorschel, R. (2022). Reconsidering digital labour. *New Technology, Work and Employment* 37(2): 288–307.

Driscoll, D. (2024). Four problems for the degrowth movement. *Jacobin*, 23 February.

Durrant, D. and Cohen, T. (2024). An infrastructural pathway to degrowth. *Democratic Theory* 11(1): 92–115.

Ejsing, M., Veng, A. and Papazu, I. (2023). Green politics beyond the state. *Climatic Change* 176(6): 73.

Ensmenger, N. (2018). The environmental history of computing. *Technology and Culture* 59(4): S7–S33.

Feola, G. (2019). Degrowth and the unmaking of capitalism. *ACME: An International Journal for Critical Geographies* 18(4): 977–97.

References

Finnegan, S. and Radloff, J. (2023). Principles of shared responsibility. AoIR2023: The 24th Annual Conference of the Association of Internet Researchers. Philadelphia, October.

Fleckenstein, P. and Dale, G. (2023). The politics of degrowth. *Tempest*, 16 August.

Flipo, F. and Schneider, F. (2015). Foreword. In D'Alisa, G., Demaria, F. and Kallis. G. (eds). *Degrowth: A Vocabulary for a New Era*. Routledge.

Floridi L. and Nobre, K (2020). The green and the blue: how AI may be a force for good. OECD, oecd-forum.org.

Fourel, C. and Corpet, O. (2012). Thinking beyond capitalism with André Gorz. *Green European Journal*, 22 October.

Fraser, N. (2022). *Cannibal Capitalism*. Verso.

Frenzel, J., Jansen, F., Liu, J., Ruddock, J., Finnegan, S. and Radloff, J. (2023). Digital infrastructures and environmental justice. Panel presented at AoIR2023: The 24th Annual Conference of the Association of Internet Researchers. Philadelphia, October.

Fuchs, C. (2008). *Internet and Society*. Routledge.

Gall, R. (2021). Tech for good is a con trick. *The Cookie*, 21 January.

Ghosh, R. (2021). The planet needs collective action – not tech. *Public Books*, 20 September.

Gibson, W. (1992). Quoted in Rosenberg, S. Virtual reality check: digital daydreams, cyberspace nightmares. *San Francisco Examiner*, 19 April, sec. Style, p. C1.4.

Golumbia, D. (2024). *Cyberlibertarianism*. University of Minnesota Press.

González, R. (2024). *How Big Tech and Silicon Valley are Transforming the Military-Industrial Complex*. White paper, 24 April. Brown University, Watson Institute for International and Public Affairs, https://watson.brown.edu.

Gorz, A. (2011). *Critique of Economic Reason*. Verso.

Gregg, M. and Strengers, Y. (2024). Getting beyond net zero dashboards in the information technology sector. *Energy Research & Social Science* 108: 103397.

Grindle, M. (2023). Permacomputing: tackling the problem of technological waste. *The New Climate*, 31 July, medium.com.

Griscom, D. (2022). Degrowth isn't realism, it's a pessimistic belief. Twitter, 12 August, https://twitter.com/DavidGriscom/status/155783 2453808705536?s=20&t=e88OTtpYNOwOndZOLjsXCA.

Haucke, F. (2018). Smartphone-enabled social change: evidence from the Fairphone case? *Journal of Cleaner Production*, 197:1719–1730.

Heikkilä, V. [aka VizNut] (2021). Permacomputing update, http://viz nut.fi/texts-en/permacomputing_update_2021.html.

References

Heikkurinen, P. (2018). Degrowth by means of technology? *Journal of Cleaner Production* 197: 1654–65.

Helfrich, S. and Bollier, D. (2015). Commons. In D'Alisa, G., Demaria, F. and Kallis. G. (eds). *Degrowth: A Vocabulary for a New Era*. Routledge.

Hickel, J. (2021). *Less is More*. Penguin.

Hickel, J. (2023). On technology and degrowth. *Monthly Review* 75(3).

Hickel, J. and Sullivan, D. (2024). How much growth is required to achieve good lives for all? Insights from needs-based analysis. *World Development Perspectives* 35: 100612.

Hickel, J., Kallis, G., Jackson, T., O'Neill, D., Schor, J., Steinberger, J., Victor, P. and Ürge-Vorsatz, D. (2022). Degrowth can work – here's how science can help. *Nature* 612, pp. 400–3.

Howson, P., Crandall, J. and Balaguer Rasillo, X. (2021). Digital degrowth innovation. *Political Geography* 88: 102415.

Huber, M. (2023). The problem with degrowth. *Jacobin*, 16 July.

Hughes, T. (1983). *Networks of Power: Electrification in Western Society, 1880–1930*. Johns Hopkins University Press.

Illich, I. (1971). *Deschooling Society*. Harper & Row.

Illich, I. (1973). *Tools for Conviviality*. Harper & Row.

Illich, Ivan (1974). *Energy and Equity*. Harper & Row.

Irimia-Vladu, M. (2014). Green electronics. *Chemical Society Reviews* 43(2): 588–610.

Jackson, S, Pompe, A. and Krieshok, G. (2012). Repair worlds. In *Proceedings of the ACM 2012 Conference on Computer Supported Cooperative Work*, pp. 107–16.

Jansen, F. (2023). The problem is growth. In Cath, C. (ed.). *Eaten by the Internet*. Meatspace Press, pp. 57–63.

Jansen, F., Gülmez, M., Kazansky, B., Abou Bakari, N., Fernandez, C., Kingaby, H. and Mühlberg, J. (2023). The climate crisis is a digital rights crisis. In *Ninth Computing within Limits 2023*, doi.org/10.21 428/bf6fb269.b4704652.

Johnson, S. (2018). The technological fix as social cure-all. *IEEE Technology and Society Magazine* 37(1): 47–54.

Josephson, C., Weitao, S., Marcano, G., Pannuto, P., Hester, J. and Wells, G. (2022). The future of clean computing may be dirty. *GetMobile: Mobile Computing and Communications* 26(3): 9–15.

Joshi, K (2023). Twitter, 19 July, https://twitter.com/KetanJ0/status/1681392736769802240.

Jyothi, A. (2023). This project cuts emissions by putting data centres inside wind turbines. *CNN Online*, 5 December, edition.cnn.com.

Kallis, G., Demaria, F. and D'Alisa, G. (2015). Introduction. In D'Alisa, G., Demaria, F. and Kallis, G. (eds). *Degrowth: A Vocabulary for a New Era*. Routledge.

References

Kallis, G., Mastini, R. and Zografos, C. (2023). Perceptions of degrowth in the European Parliament. *Nature Sustainability* 7(1): 1–9.

Kallis, G., Paulson, S., D'Alisa, G. and Demaria, F. (2020). *The Case for Degrowth*. Polity.

Kerschner, C., Wächter, P., Nierling, L. and Ehlers, M. (2018). Degrowth and technology. *Journal of Cleaner Production* 197: 1619–36.

Kidron, M. (1966). Some trees, no wood. *International Socialism* 24, marxists.org.

Kinder, J. (2023). Ambivalence and intensity. In Pasek, A., Lin, C., Griffin, Z., Cooper, T. and Kinder, J. (eds). *Digital Energetics*. University of Minnesota Press.

Kitchin, R. and Fraser, A. (2020). *Slow Computing*. Bristol University Press.

Kneese, T. (2023). Climate justice and labour rights. AI Now Institute, http://dx.doi.org/10.2139/ssrn.4533853.

Kolbert, E. (2024). The obscene energy demands of AI. *The New Yorker*, 9 March.

Kostakis, V. (2024). What technology for degrowth? *Resilience*, 13 March.

Kostakis, V. and Tsiouris, N. (2024). How to unite local initiatives for a more sustainable global future. *Sustainable Futures* 7: 100187.

Kostakis, V., Niaros, V. and Giotitsas, C. (2023). Beyond global versus local. *Sustainability Science* 18(5): 2309–22.

Kostakis, V., Pazaitis, A. and Liarokapis, M. (2023). Beyond high-tech versus low-tech. *Big Data & Society* 10(1): 20539517231180583.

Kroeker, L. (2022). African Renaissance, Afrotopia, Afropolitanism and Afrofuturism. *Africa Spectrum* 57(2): 113–33.

Kwet, M. (2024). *Digital Degrowth: Technology in the Age of Survival*. Pluto.

Ladino, J. (2012). *Reclaiming Nostalgia*. University of Virginia Press.

Lage, J., Thema, J., Zell-Ziegler, C., Best, B., Cordroch, L. and Wiese, F. (2023). Citizens call for sufficiency and regulation. *Energy Research & Social Science* 104: 103254.

Latouche, S. (2009). *Farewell to Growth*. Polity.

Lenzen, T. (2024). Champions of degrowth want to shrink the economy to save the world. *New York Times*, 8 June.

Levy, S. (1984). *Hackers: Heroes of the Computer Revolution*. Press/ Doubleday.

Li, P., Yang, J., Islam, M. and Ren, S. (2023). Making AI less 'thirsty', https://arxiv.org/pdf/2304.03271.

Liegey, V. and Nelson, A. (2020). *Exploring Degrowth*. Pluto.

Likavcan, L. and Scholz-Wackerle, M. (2018). Technology appropriation in a de-growing economy. *Journal of Cleaner Production* 197: 1666–75.

130 References

Lucia, B., Balaji, V., Colin, A., Maeng, K. and Ruppel, E. (2017). Intermittent computing: challenges and opportunities. 2nd Summit on Advances in Programming Languages (SNAPL 2017).

McAfee, A. (2020). Why degrowth is the worst idea on the planet. *Wired*, 6 October.

McIlwain, C. (2019). *Black Software*. Oxford University Press.

McQuillan, D. (2025). Environmental peacebuilding and AI. *Environment and Security*, https://research.gold.ac.uk/id/eprint/37338.

Madianou, M. (2021). Nonhuman humanitarianism. *Information, Communication and Society* 24(6): 850–68.

Magalhães, J. and Couldry, N. (2021). Giving by taking away. *International Journal of Communication* 15: 343–62.

March, H. (2018). The smart city and other ICT-led techno-imaginaries. *Journal of Cleaner Production* 197: 1694–1703.

Marquis, C. (2024). In defence of degrowth. *Harvard Business Review*, 11 June.

Maxwell, R. and Miller, T. (2020). *How Green is Your Smartphone?* Polity.

Meadows, D. H., Meadows, D. L., Randers, J. and Behrens, W. (1972). *The Limits to Growth*. Club of Rome.

Microsoft/PwC (2019). How AI can enable a sustainable future, https://www.pwc.co.uk/services/sustainability-climate-change/insights/how-ai-future-can-enable-sustainable-future.html.

Miller, T. (2015). The internet of things will be an internet of obsolete junk. *The Conversation*, 28 January.

Moore, J. (2021). The rise of cheap nature. In Aloi, G. and McHugh, S. (eds). *Posthumanism in Art and Science*. Columbia University Press, pp. 301–7.

Morell, M. (2015). Digital commons. In D'Alisa, G., Demaria, F. and Kallis. G. (eds). *Degrowth: A Vocabulary for a New Era*. Routledge.

Morozov, E. (2013). *To Save Everything, Click Here*. PublicAffairs.

Mulgan, G. (2013). *The Locust and the Bee*. Princeton University Press.

Munn, L. (2024). The five tests: designing and evaluating AI according to indigenous Māori principles. *AI & Society* 39(4): 1673–81.

Mytton, D. (2021). Data centre water consumption. *npj Clean Water* 4, Article number: 11.

New Climate Institute (2022). *Corporate Climate Responsibility Monitor 2022*, newclimate.org

O'Brien, M. and Fingerhut, H. (2023). AI tools fuelled a 34% spike in Microsoft's water consumption, and one city with its data centres is concerned about the effect on residential supply. *Fortune*, 10 September.

References

Pansera, M., Ehlers, M. and Kerschner, C. (2019). Unlocking wise digital techno-futures. *Futures* 114: 102474.

Pansera, M. and Fressoli, M. (2021). Innovation without growth. *Organization* 28(3): 380–404.

Pansera, M., Lloveras, J. and Durrant, D. (2024). The infrastructural conditions of (de-)growth. *Ecological Economics* 215: 108001.

Pargman, D. (2015). On the limits of limits. *First Monday* 20(8).

Pargman, D. and Wallsten, B. (2017). Resource scarcity and socially just internet access over time and space. *Proceedings of the 2017 Workshop on Computing Within Limits*, pp. 29–36, doi.org/10.11 45/3080556.3084083.

Pawełczak, P. (n.d.). Intermittent computing to replace trillions of batteries. TU Delft, tudelft.nl.

Pierce, J. (2012). Undesigning technology. *Proceedings of the SIGCHI Conference on Human Factors in Computing Systems*, pp. 957–66.

Pitron, G. (2023). *The Dark Cloud*. Scribe.

Powell, A., Ustek-Spilda, F., Lehuedé, S. and Shklovski, I. (2022). Addressing ethical gaps in 'Technology for Good'. *Big Data & Society* 9(2): 20539517221113774.

Quijano, P. (2023). Resisting data colonialism. In Tierra Común Network (eds). *Resisting Data Colonialism*. Institute of Network Cultures, Amsterdam, pp. 96–7.

Radhakrishnan, R. (2021). Experiments with social good: feminist critiques of artificial intelligence in healthcare in India. *Catalyst: Feminism, Theory, Technoscience* 7(2).

Raghavan, B. and Hasan, S. (2016). Macroscopically sustainable networking. *Proceedings of the Second Workshop on Computing within Limits*, pp. 1–6, doi/10.1145/2926676.2926685.

Ramírez, P. (2023). No to the data centre! In Tierra Común Network (eds). *Resisting Data Colonialism*. Institute of Network Cultures, Amsterdam, pp. 57–62.

Rathi, A. (2024). *Climate Capitalism: Winning the Race to Zero Emissions and Solving the Crisis of our Age*. Greystone.

Richie, H. (2024). *Not the End of the World: How We Can be the First Generation to Build a Sustainable Planet*. Penguin.

Rosenberger, R. (2023). Against spectatorial utopianism. *AI & Society* 38: 1965–6.

Routledge, P., Cumbers, A. and Derickson, K. (2018). States of just transition. *Geoforum* 88: 78–86.

Ruddock, J. and Donovan, J. (2023). Towards a public interest internet. In Cath, C. (ed). *Eaten by the Internet*. Meatspace Press, pp. 117–22.

Sadowski, J. (2025). *The Mechanic and the Luddite*. University of California Press.

Sætra, H. (2023). *Technology and Sustainable Development*. Routledge.

Saitō, K. (2024). *Slow Down: The Degrowth Manifesto*. Penguin.

Samerski, S. (2018). Tools for degrowth? Ivan Illich's critique of technology revisited. *Journal of Cleaner Production* 197: 1637–46.

Santarius, T., Bieser, J., Frick, V., Höjer, M., Gossen, M., Hilty, L., Kern, E., Pohl, J., Rohde, F. and Lange, S. (2023). Digital sufficiency. *Annals of Telecommunications* 78(5): 277–95.

Schmelzer, M., Vetter, A. and Vansintjan, A. (2022). *The Future is Degrowth*. Verso.

Scholz, T. and Schneider, N. (2016). *Ours to Hack and Own*. OR Books.

Schumacher, E. (1973). *Small is Beautiful*. Harper Collins.

Schumacher, E. (1980). *Good Work*. Harper Collins.

Schütze, P. (2024). The problem of sustainable AI. *Weizenbaum Journal of the Digital Society* 4(1): w4.1.4.

Sekulova, F., Kallis, G., Rodríguez-Labajos, B. and Schneider, F. (2013). Degrowth: from theory to practice. *Journal of Cleaner Production* 38: 1–6.

Sharma, V., Kumar, N. and Nardi, B. (2023). Post-growth human–computer interaction. *ACM Transactions on Computer-Human Interaction* 31(1): 1–37.

Shew, A. (2023). *Against Technoableism*. W. W. Norton.

Shove, E. (2023). *Connecting Practices*. Routledge.

Shove, E., Pantzar, M. and Watson, M. (2012). *The Dynamics of Social Practice*. Sage.

Siddarth, D. and Nabben, K. (2021). What tech futurists get wrong about human autonomy. *Noema*, 9 December.

Smil, V. (2022). Decarbonisation algebra. *IEEE Spectrum*, February, pp. 20–1.

Soper K. (2023). *Post-growth Living*. Verso.

Speed, R. (2024). Raspberry Pi sets IPO jam for June. *The Register*, 22 May.

Staltz, A. (2021). Twitter, 3 September, https://twitter.com/andrestaltz/status/1433782103183872000.

Statista (2024). Personal computing devices shipments worldwide from 2024 to 2028. https://www.statista.com/statistics/272595/global-shipments-forecast-for-tablets-laptops-and-desktop-pcs.

Steele C. (2021). *Digital Black Feminism*. New York University Press.

Stokel-Walker, C. (2023). Turns out there's another problem with AI – its environmental toll. *The Guardian*, 1 August.

Strand, R., Saltelli, A., Giampietro, M., Rommetveit, K. and Funtowicz, S. (2018). New narratives for innovation. *Journal of Cleaner Production* 197: 1849–53.

References

Strunk, B. (2023). Between limits and abundance. *Degrowth Journal* 1: 00028.

Sutherland, B. (2022). Strategies for degrowth computing. *Eighth Workshop on Computing within Limits*, June, https://computing withinlimits.org/2022/papers/limits22-final-Sutherland.pdf.

Taffel, S. (2025). Fantasies of dematerialization: (un)sustainable growth and digital capitalism. In Certomà, C., Iapaolo, F. and Martellozzo, F. (eds). *Digital Technologies for Sustainable Futures: Promises and Pitfalls*. Routledge.

Templin, S. (2021). Design for disassembly, *Core* 77, 20 July, core77.com/posts.

Todd, J. (2012). From deschooling to unschooling. In Haworth, R. (ed.), *Anarchist Pedagogies*. PM Press, pp. 69–87.

Tomlinson, B. (n.d). Collapse informatics, http://postgrowth.art/collapse-informatics-En.html.

Tonkinwise, C. (2018). I prefer not to: anti-progressive designing. In Coombs, G., McNamara, A. and Sade, G. (eds.) (2019). *Undesign: Critical Practices at the Intersection of Art and Design*. Routledge, pp.74–84.

Toupin, S. (2024). Shaping feminist artificial intelligence. *New Media & Society* 26(1): 580–95.

Turner, F. (2006). *From Counterculture to Cyberculture*. University of Chicago Press.

Valdivia, A. (2022). Silicon Valley and the environmental costs of AI. Political Economy and Research Centre, 5 December, perc.org.uk.

Vallor, S. (2022). We used to get excited about technology – what happened? *MIT Technology Review*, 21 October.

Van Chinh, T., Mastantuoni, G., Zabihipour, M., Li, L., Berglund, L., Berggren, M., Zhou, Q. and Engquist, I. (2023). Electrical current modulation in wood electrochemical transistor. *Proceedings of the National Academy of Sciences* 120(18): e2218380120.

Vanderbauwhede, W. (2021). Low carbon and sustainable computing. 29 June, https://www.dcs.gla.ac.uk/~wim/low-carbon-computing.

Vetter, A. (2018). The matrix of convivial technology. *Journal of Cleaner Production* 197: 1778–86.

Wainwright, J. and Mann, G. (2018). *Climate Leviathan*. Verso.

Waring, B. (2021). There aren't enough trees in the world to offset society's carbon emissions – and there never will be. *The Conversation*, 23 April.

Washington, H., Chapron, G., Kopnina, H., Curry, P., Gray, J. and Piccolo, J. (2018). Foregrounding ecojustice in conservation. *Biological Conservation* 228: 367–74.

Washington Post (2021). Americans widely distrust Facebook, TikTok and Instagram with their data, poll finds. 22 December.

Weinberger, S. (2017). *The Imagineers of War*. Vintage.

Wellner, G. and Rothman, T. (2020). Feminist AI. *Philosophy & Technology* 33(2): 191–205.

White, R. and Williams, C. (2016). Beyond capitalocentricism. *Area* 48: 325–31.

Whittaker, M. (2023). Twitter, 23 November, https://twitter.com/mer_edith/status/1727334747129487686.

Winner, L. (1980). Do artefacts have politics?. *Daedalus* 109(1): 121–36.

Winner, L. (1997). Cyberlibertarian myths and the prospects for community. *Computers and Society* 27(3): 14–19.

Woodridge, A. (2013). The coming tech-lash. *The Economist*, 18 November.

Wright, E. (2010). *Envisioning Real Utopias*. Verso.

Zuckerberg, M. (2012). Letter to shareholders from Mark Zuckerberg. Reprinted in *The Financial Times*, 12 February.

Index

activism 9, 22, 46, 68, 82, 94–5, 98, 120

AI (artificial intelligence) 2, 4, 6, 9, 12, 24, 25, 26, 30–1, 34, 35, 39, 58, 64, 69, 80, 112, 120

air travel 13, 62

Amazon 3, 31, 39, 117

Andreessen, Marc 55, 71

Apple 31, 117

autonomy 52–3, 59, 80, 84, 91, 117

Berners-Lee, Tim 10, 65

bicycles 60–1, 64

Big Tech 3–5, 25–6, 31, 34, 36–8, 58, 64–5, 77, 81, 82, 109, 118–19, 121

biodegradable computing 101–2

capitalist / capitalism 18–23, 30, 33, 35, 36, 42–5, 48–9, 51, 56, 61–4, 68, 72, 76–7, 80, 81, 87, 95, 108–9, 121

carbon (offsetting) 33–4, 36, 37

carbon emissions/footprint 13, 14, 24, 30, 33, 34, 35, 36, 70

care 20, 21, 22, 42, 43, 44, 49, 50, 52–3, 56, 61, 68, 90, 105

cars 20, 49, 61, 63, 70, 78, 112

Chat GPT 4, 14

China 3, 4, 13, 120

citizen assemblies 79–80, 82

climate change/collapse/crisis 15, 29, 30, 31, 34, 35, 42, 45, 54, 80, 105, 120, 121

commons 51, 53, 65, 73, 78, 80, 84–6, 88, 89, 90, 92, 109, 115

communitarian 85, 108

community 10, 19, 21, 28, 43, 47–9, 50–3, 55, 60, 64, 67, 70, 73, 74, 80–4, 89–95, 111, 112, 115, 116–17, 120

Computing Within Limits 68, 95, 98

conviviality 22, 51–3, 59, 60, 65, 73, 87, 91–3, 113

data centres 3, 12, 13, 15, 31, 32, 34, 35, 39, 78, 81, 91, 112, 122

degrowth, criticisms of 53–5

Index

deliberative democracy 79–80, 110
digital divide 8, 14
digital resignation 7, 51
digital sufficiency 69–73, 79, 95
discrimination 9, 11, 24

e-waste 3, 11, 13, 14, 33, 36, 42, 45, 89, 105
enshittification 10–11

Facebook 10, 26, 117
free software 84–6, 89
frugal computing 70, 87, 96–7
fungal computing 103–4

Google 5, 12, 14, 19, 20, 25, 26, 29, 39, 78, 81, 108, 117
Gorz, André 45, 85
grassroots 59, 59, 65, 110, 116, 120
Green Tech 22, 32, 34–6, 38–40, 62, 108
Gregg, Mel 34
growth 16–19, 23, 31, 32, 34, 45, 47, 56, 62, 69, 108, 109, 110

Hickel, Jason 46, 47, 61–3, 75

Illich, Ivan 22, 51, 52, 59, 64, 65, 72, 113
Indigenous/First Nations 45, 56, 81
infrastructure 3, 8, 11, 12, 19, 26, 45, 51, 52, 58, 61, 66, 67, 69, 78, 90–1, 97, 98, 100, 104, 105, 109, 114, 119
intermittent computing 66, 101
investment 15, 16, 18, 20, 21, 28, 43, 47, 109

Jansen, Fieke 19, 39, 98, 109

Kallis, Giorgos 46, 48, 49, 52, 78, 116, 119, 121
Kneese, Tamara 13, 33, 36

labour 4, 12, 15, 19, 42, 78
libraries 60, 67, 80, 89, 90, 113, 116

material/materiality 1, 3, 4, 11, 13, 15, 31, 33, 41, 42, 45, 47, 54, 59, 60, 73, 89, 90, 98, 99, 102, 103, 104, 106, 114, 115, 122
mesh networks 91, 97
Microsoft 3, 12, 17, 30, 31, 108
military, origins of tech 19–21, 58, 62, 110
modular devices 88–9, 111
mycelium 103–4, 106

net zero 31, 34–6, 127

off-grid 67, 100
open source 84–5, 86
optimization 17, 99

permacomputing 69, 72, 95
planned obsolescence 13, 17, 72, 80, 88, 96
pollution 11, 13, 30
post-capitalist 20, 23, 48, 54, 85, 120, 122
protest 77, 80–1
public opinion 77–9

radically sustainable computing 68, 95–7
rare metals / minerals 1, 3, 11, 12, 102, 104
Raspberry Pi 86–7, 92
recycling 13, 63, 89, 96
repair 48, 52, 58, 60, 63, 67–70, 74, 77, 79, 82, 87–90, 92, 103, 110, 111, 113, 116, 120, 121

Index

resistance 80–1, 118
right to repair 79, 87, 88, 110, 119

Saitō, Kōhei 46, 52, 117
salvage 13, 23, 58, 96–7, 98, 105, 122
scalability 17, 19, 32, 90, 91
schools 2, 80, 89, 112, 113, 116
self-determinism 48, 50, 52, 72, 90, 116
semiconductor 19, 20, 98, 102
sensors 99, 101
sharing 48, 52, 60, 65, 85, 86, 87, 88, 90, 91, 110, 111, 113
Silicon Valley 10, 19, 20, 26, 37, 43, 55, 71
simplicity 46–7, 79
single board computers 86–7

slow computing 69–70
smartphones 1, 2, 3, 5, 6, 7, 9, 11, 13, 14, 64, 81, 86, 88, 89, 90, 104, 115
solutionism 6, 24, 25, 26, 30, 33, 34, 37
Soper, Kate 32, 37
supply chains 3, 13, 15, 31, 60
sustainability 25, 29, 32, 34, 37, 38, 39, 41, 55, 98, 105, 108, 117, 118, 119, 122

Tech for Good 22, 25, 26–9, 35–8, 40, 108
tech workers 81–2, 118

water 11, 12, 14, 31, 33, 34, 37, 54, 67, 81, 99, 100, 103–5
Winner, Langdon 15–16, 85